Children
Mourning

Mourning
Children

Children
Mourning
Mourning
Children

Edited by
Kenneth J. Doka, Ph.D.

HFA

Hospice Foundation of America

Ordering information:

Bookstores and individuals order additional copies from:
    Taylor & Francis
    1900 Frost Road, Suite 101
    Bristol, PA 19007

To order by phone, call toll free 1-800-821-8312
or send orders on a 24-hour telefax, 215-785-5515
Orders can be placed via Internet at bkorders@tandfpa.com

For bulk quantity orders, call Hospice Foundation of America,
1-800-854-3402
or write:
    Hospice Foundation of America
    Suite 300
    2001 S Street, NW
    Washington, DC 20009

Book design and cover by New Age Graphics, Bethesda, MD
Typesetting by Edington-Rand, Inc. Riverdale, MD

Library of Congress Cataloging-in-Print data available upon request.

ISBN: 1-56032-447-3

Table of Contents

Foreword

Jack D. Gordon
President, Hospice Foundation of America

In March 1994, the Hospice Foundation of America sponsored a teleconference called *Living With Grief: Personally and Profession-ally.* We had expected to reach possibly 2,500-3,000 caregivers, primarily those involved professionally with hospices across the country. We thought 50 downlinks was a reasonable, and satisfactory, goal. To our delighted surprise, more than 900 institutions — hospices, hospitals, community colleges, public television stations, among others — sponsored a downlink in their communities and, as a result, our audience exceeded 40,000 people. Beyond the continental United States, we were seen in Hawaii, Alaska, Puerto Rico and in Canada.

Cokie Roberts of ABC News generously agreed to moderate a small panel of academic-practitioners gathered with the advice of Dr. Kenneth Doka, then president of the Association for Death Education and Counseling, a professor of gerontology at the College of New Rochelle, and a Lutheran minister. The teleconference, informal, interactive, and instructive, in addition to being praised by its audience elicited several thousand applications for continuing education credit. It was, in short, a gratifying success far beyond our expectations.

What was an even greater surprise to us came later. When the evaluation forms began to flow in, the section inviting suggestions for future programs was heavy with the recommendation that we focus this year on children and grief. On the surface that seemed a bit strange. While we had previously worked with hospices, hospitals, and nursing home staff in their work with children, including pediatric AIDS cases, only a tiny percentage — less than one percent — of hospice patients are, in fact, children.

Beneath the surface, however, there was the obvious fact that all of us are or have been children at one time and many of us, whatever our age, have parents who are still alive, but who are getting older. The problems of grief and bereavement when a child of whatever age dies or when a parent or sibling dies are immensely troublesome. There is clearly much information that needs to be shared. One hospice worker noted, "We deal with children and grandchildren all the time, yet we are trained to deal primarily with the elderly and terminally-ill. Children may not be patients in our hospice program, but they are certainly part of our responsibility. As we support them, we really do serve our patients as well. Help us help them."

We followed the suggestion of our participants. We asked Ken Doka to advise us again on this year's conference and with his guidance we have put together an effort which, as I write this, is much farther along than last year at the same time, leading us to expect closer to 1,500 downlinks and possibly 60,000 participants this year. We have had to turn down potential site sponsors in England, Germany, Italy, Turkey, Spain, and the Azores since we had no money left in our teleconference budget for an international satellite. One of the reasons is this book.

Last year, we reprinted several excerpts from panelists work in our program book. The excerpts were fine, as far as they went, but participants once again became advisers. They urged us to expand the written material so that they would have a document for further study. They wanted a longer-lasting basic resource and this book is the result. People who will appear on the panel and several others in the field have contributed original papers, and several research papers of note have also been included.

We aimed to produce something between a popular self-help book and an academic tome, a readable book directed primarily at caregivers, but which might also benefit a family dealing with a pediatric-related problem of grief and bereavement. We hope that *Children Mourning, Mourning Children* will find an audience beyond those who receive it at the teleconference. We look forward to its continued use in training, counseling, and study.

The teleconference and the book, we believe, fit comfortably with our mission "to provide leadership in the development and application of hospice and its philosophy of care for terminally ill people, with the goal of enhancing the American health care system and the role of hospice within it."

The Hospice Foundation of America has grown with the hospice movement in the United States. We began in 1982. receiving most of our money, then as now, from people who have had some contact with hospice, generally through a family member who was in the program. To a lesser extent, we have also benefited from grants from civic and fraternal groups, other foundations, corporations, and associations.

In recent years, we have, in turn, made small grants or supported programs over a wide range of hospice-related issues. We have encouraged the training of physicians in pain and symptom control and have supported a pastoral intern program to train clergy in hospice ways. We have financed studies and conferences on ethical questions at the end-of-life and on the comparative cost of hospice as opposed to hospital care. We have made grants to a number of hospices for a variety of local educational and informational programs.

This year we have also underwritten a monthly newsletter, *Journeys: A Newsletter to Help in Bereavement*, which several hundred hospices, and other organizations, are sending to the families of their patients. Thousands of grieving people have begun to benefit from the quietly friendly counsel it contains.

We hope you find this book a useful source of information. We would welcome any suggestions for future teleconferences and publications. We are proud to be able to produce the teleconference on its merit alone, but we are also pleased that it is such a cost-effective way of communicating with caring people all across the country. The cost to the Hospice Foundation will this year exceed $200,000, a cost per viewer of under $4. As we look forward to our continued work and the special niche we have found, we certainly welcome any individual, corporate, or foundation contribution that will permit us to do better what we have begun.

Grief and bereavement know no boundaries of age, gender, or place. Where there is a sense of isolation, we want to be there directly through our written documents and through our video presentations and indirectly through caregivers. Where there is a yearning to help others, we want to do what we can to make that help as appropriate as we can. Where there is a sense of sadness, we want to be able to offer a hand that moves sadness aside. Where there is pain, we hope to bring comfort. That is, we think, the essence of the hospice movement.

Preface

This book, edited for the Hospice Foundation's second annual "Living With Grief: Children Mourning, Mourning Children" teleconference is compiled with two purposes in mind. First, it serves as a source book for the teleconference, providing remarks from conference speakers, as well as other caregivers and researchers in the field, that might allow participants opportunities for exploring in more depth the topics so briefly broached. Second, I hope it can serve as a brief, useful introduction for educators and caregivers.

As with any edited book, there are innumerable overlaps, complicated here by the looming teleconference deadline. Yet taken together, I think these chapters offer a powerful affirmation and exploration of three basic and significant themes.

1. Children are always developing. Therefore, their understandings of death and their reactions to illness and loss also are undergoing change.

There is a tendency to see child development in cognitive terms. At what age can children understand death? At what age should they be allowed to attend a funeral?

The chapters in this book affirm that development is always multifaceted. Children are not only developing physically (which is the most evident), or cognitively, but spiritually, emotionally, socially, psychologically and behaviorally as well. Their cultural and religious background, the supports available to them within their families, communities and schools as well their life experiences differ. Hence there are no ready and easy answers to the questions previously posed.

Rather, one needs to understand children as constantly developing and trying to make sense of their world and the events that are occurring to and around them. At different phases in development, the same event, such as an illness, may pose different challenges and problems. But at each phase, children both need to utilize their own inherent strengths, and, though they may express it differently, the support both of peers and adults.

2. Children grieve in ways that are both different from and similar to adults.

Throughout the field of death studies, there has been a recurring debate over when children reach a level of developmental maturity when they are capable of recognizing and experiencing loss. To many, the answer is that children at any age can recognize loss though they may respond to it in different ways. A number of the chapters here remind caregivers that children may not always verbalize their sense of loss or demonstrate it in traditional patterns of grief. They may act out or regress. Their grief may be expressed in anger, accidents or sleep disturbances or their grief can become expressed through physical symptoms. The heartache becomes expressed as a head or stomach ache.

They may need different therapeutic approaches than adults. Natural, or expressive therapies such as music, art, play, dance, or drama can not only be cathartic, projective and reflective, but can also seem less threatening than talking one-on-one with an adult. And since children are unable to sustain strong emotions for a longer period, shorter, more intensive sessions may be helpful. Children may revisit early losses. It is not unusual for children as they grow to regrieve losses experienced early in childhood. For as they age their dimensions of that loss may be more clearly understood.

But there are also similarities. Like adults, each loss is different. The grief experience will be affected by many of the same factors that affect adults—the nature and quality of the relationships, the availability of support, the circumstances of the loss, the psychological resilience and coping skills of the child, as well as social variables such as class, gender, religion and culture.

3. Children need significant support as they deal with loss.

Since they are struggling with their own developmental issues and emerging strengths, children will need help in dealing with significant loss. This is especially problematic since the adults in their immediate circle may themselves be grieving. But as the chapters affirm, there are many sources of help. Caregivers, peers, educators, funeral directors, counselors and clinicians can all play critical and supportive roles. The challenge for the parent then is that when they cannot provide support, they need to empower it.

There is one other comment that ought to appear as part of this preface. Talking to children about loss and illness is too important to be left to a crisis. Rather it is helpful to provide opportunities for children to discuss loss in times that are not so emotionally laden. Reading stories, watching television and videos such as *Charlotte's Web*, or even watching leaves bud, color and fall all provide opportunities for children to begin to encounter loss. Such occasions can have many roles. They open communication between parents and the child, reassuring the child that nothing is too threatening to discuss. They can lead to skills and understandings that are essentials to the child for coping with loss. And they can reaffirm that death is part of the process of living.

Dedication

To all children who mourn,
to all those who mourn children, and
to all those who care for them.

Acknowledgements

It has always been my style to thank those who contributed to this work, both directly and indirectly. First, I want to thank the Hospice Foundation of America, its president Jack Gordon, and its vice presidents David Abrams and Norman Sherman for their vision in making both book and teleconference so readily available resources. Norman Sherman and Diane and Barry Eisenberg have been patient taskmasters throughout this project. I would also like to thank all the contributors to this book. They probably did not find me that patient a taskmaster. In addition, my secretary Rosemary Strobel and my graduate assistants Maura Curry and Lynn Wohland have, as always, been invaluable.

The Association for Death Education and Counseling, a co-sponsor of the teleconference, remains a continued source of colleagues, stimulation and support. And, I appreciate the constant support provided by the Graduate School of the College of New Rochelle as well as the ongoing stimulation offered by my students. Finally, I want to acknowledge both the understanding and necessary distractions offered by Kathy, Mike, Shawn, and Devin, those who are much a part of my life and home.

K.D.
Poughkeepsie, N.Y.

♦

Section One
The Child's Perspective of Death

In order to understand the ways that children respond to life-threatening illness or to experiences of death, it is essential to understand first how children develop an understanding of the concept of death. Charles Corr's chapter provides such an overview.

Corr makes a number of essential points that will be echoed throughout the book. First, Corr reminds us that cognitive development is deeply affected by the child's experiences and culture. This is a critical point. It is easy to get caught up in discussions of what the child can or cannot understand. In fact, cognitive developmental perspectives have been criticized since they often overstress what the child is capable of understanding rather than that the child is actively *trying* to make sense of the world even within the limits of his or her cognitive capabilities. Corr reaffirms both that chronological age is a highly limited way to understand cognitive development and that a child's perspective and understanding of death will be significantly influenced by the ways the child's culture understands death as well as the child's own life experiences.

Corr also emphasizes that while the child is developing cognitively he/she is also developing behaviorally, socially, physically, and spiritually. Loss and life-threatening illness will affect each form of development. For example, Robert Coles (1990) in his work on the spiritual development of children describes children as spiritual pilgrims or pioneers, traveling in new places, sometimes beyond their own cognitive mappings, to find meaning in illness, death and loss. Similarly, David Crenshaw (1991) reminds us that younger children not only may have shorter attention spans but a "short feeling span" as well. Frequently, they are unable to cope with strong emotions for long periods of time. Their moods then may change quickly. Their behaviors too may be disconnected to social expectations about how they should feel or act. The angry acting-out child can be just as distraught as the crying child. Understanding then the broad process of child development enhances our perspective of the ways to comprehend and assist the child facing loss.

That translation has always been Earl Grollman's great strength. In his chapter, Grollman continues to explore the ways understanding adults can assist the child at the child's level. But Grollman also reminds us that compassion must always join understanding as the child copes with loss.

References

Coles, Robert. (1990). *The Spiritual Life of Children*. Boston, MA: Houghton Mifflin.

Crenshaw, David. (1991). *Bereavement: Counseling The Bereaved Throughout The Life Cycle*. NY: Continuum.

Children's Understandings of Death

1

Striving to Understand Death

Charles A. Corr

In an audiovisual by the same title (Encyclopedia Britannica Films, 1975, 19 minutes), a child asks the question: *"Where is dead?"* Clearly, this is not a typical adult question. It does not frame the issue in ways with which adults are familiar or comfortable. But that does not make it a bad question. A child's efforts to understand death are no less real or forceful simply because they may seem strange or puzzling to adults.

In this case, the child went on to say: *"Where do you go when you're dead?"* Now we see more clearly some main directions in the child's thinking. And we can note some assumptions: that there is a "you" following death; that there is a "where" involved in death; and that the "you" engages in a process of going to that "(some)-where."

An adult might "answer" these questions by saying, "Nowhere." That may only lead the child to ask, "But where is that?" A moral is that adults must enter with care into a child's world if we are to know how to appreciate and respond effectively to that child's understandings (and concerns) about death.

This chapter focuses on issues related to children's understandings of death. Our discussion covers five major points:

1. the principal elements that enter into children's understandings of death;
2. some questions that children frequently ask in their efforts to comprehend those elements of the concept of death;
3. some comparisons between younger and older children's understandings of death;
4. some contrasts between stage-based and task-based approaches in seeking to explain children's understandings of death; and

5. some suggestions about how this work of understanding death is linked to children's tasks in coping with loss, grief, and life-threatening illness.

Understanding the Concept of Death: Five Principal Subconcepts

Striving to achieve an understanding of the concept of death is a difficult challenge for all human beings, and perhaps even more so for children. One important reason for this difficulty is that the concept of death is not a simple, uncomplicated notion. In fact, it embraces several subconcepts or components. Each of these subconcepts is a central element in what children tell us about their master concepts of death. Some of these subconcepts have their own subordinate components or elements.

Speece and Brent (in press) recently reviewed more than 100 research studies conducted between 1934 and the early 1990s to investigate children's understandings of death. Their review revealed that there are at least four and perhaps five principal subconcepts involved in children's concepts of death. These subconcepts are:

1. universality;
2. irreversibility;
3. nonfunctionality;
4. causality; and
5. some type of continued life form.

(1) Universality

When children attempt to grasp the subconcept of "universality" in their understandings of death, they are challenged to comprehend what is involved in recognizing that *all living things must eventually die.* This involves bringing into their thinking *three closely-related notions:*

a. all inclusiveness;
b. inevitability; and
c. unpredictability.

(a) All inclusiveness. The notion of "all inclusiveness" has to do with the extent of the group of living things to which the concept of death applies. Does the concept of death apply to some, many, most, or absolutely all living things?

(b) Inevitability. The notion of "inevitability" has to do with the *necessity* with which death applies to living things. If the scope of death is all inclusive for living things, is its force so compelling or powerful as to make it inevitable?

Many children are aware that particular individuals can and do sometimes avoid particular causes of death. For example, in children's cartoons on television and in real life, familiar persons may evade or be resuscitated from a specific threat of death. If so, the challenge in grasping the inevitability of death as an aspect of its universality is to understand that, despite one's awareness that death has been or can be avoided in specific cases, no living individual can ultimately avoid death indefinitely.

(c) Unpredictability. The notion of "unpredictability" is a third and apparently paradoxical element associated with the universality of death. If death is absolutely all inclusive and inevitable, a child might reasonably conclude that its *timing* would also be certain and predictable. In fact, that is not the case. Achieving an understanding of the universality of death includes grasping the notion that death is an inevitable but not a predictable outcome in the lives of living things.

(2) Irreversibility

When children attempt to grasp the subconcept of "irreversibility" in their understandings of death, they are challenged to comprehend what is involved in recognizing that once the physical body of a living thing is dead, it can never be alive again. Irreversibility is one aspect of what is meant by the "finality" of death. But "finality" can indicate both "irreversibility" and "nonfunctionality" (see below). So perhaps it is better to think of irreversibility in terms of "irrevocability" or "permanence."

Speece and Brent (in press) have explained that irreversibility involves both the *processes* which distinguish the transition from being alive to being dead and the state which results from them. Thus, the unconditional irreversibility of death means that the physical body can no longer be restored to its former life.

Note that everything asserted here about understanding the concept of death and its various subconcepts excludes two considerations which might occur to children, but which are really outside the scope of this concept. First, we are discussing natural processes or states. *Miraculous or magical events and explanations* are excluded from this account by definition. As supernatural possibilities, they would (if they really did or could occur) go beyond ordinary human understanding and are not considered here.

Second, in recent times *medical resuscitation* has complicated the subconcept of irreversibility. But that only means that there is a kind of boundary region between being alive and being dead, a region of ambiguity within which a person may be incapable of autonomous cardiopulmonary functioning but from which resuscitation may be possible. If so, the person has not crossed the final boundary to death, a state from which life in the physical body is irreversibly absent.

(3) Nonfunctionality

When children attempt to grasp the subconcept of "nonfunctionality" in their understandings of death, they are challenged to comprehend that once a living thing is dead, all of the life-defining capabilities or functional capacities that are typically attributed to a living physical body cease. This is the second aspect of the "finality" of death. "Irreversibility" refers to the inability to reverse the processes and the state involved in death; "non-functionality" refers to the final cessation of bodily functions.

Life-defining functions that children typically attribute to a living human being are of two types:

1. external or observable functions, such as breathing, eating, walking, or playing; and
2. internal functions which are not directly observed but are inferred from what is observed or expected of a living thing, such as feeling, thinking, or dreaming.

Nonfunctionality includes the cessation of both external and internal functions.

There is widespread agreement among researchers about these first three subconcepts as aspects of the master concept of death. But two other subconcepts also deserve attention here.

(4) Causality

When children attempt to grasp the subconcept of "causality" in their understandings of death, they are challenged to comprehend what it is that really does or can bring about the death of a living thing. For example, children frequently suggest "magical" causes, such as bad behavior or wishing that someone would die, and "specific" or "individual" causes, such as an unusual event that caused a particular death and is restricted to that individual situation, such as being killed by a television character.

Some researchers (e.g., Speece and Brent, in press) believe that a mature understanding of the subconcept of causality involves an *abstract* (or generalizable) and *realistic* understanding of both external and internal events that might bring about death. This view suggests that to comprehend the causality of death, one must understand that death can result from external causes, but that even when such outside factors are not present it will ultimately result from internal causes (or at least from a combination of external and internal causes). Furthermore, this view might claim that merely naming "old age" does not indicate an adequate grasp of the causality of death since old age on its own is not a specific cause of death. Note that adults in our society and in other cultures do not always agree on what is involved in a fully-developed understanding of the causality of death.

(5) Some Type of Continued Life Form

Research by Brent and Speece (1993) has shown that both children and adults commonly report as a part of their concept of death an understanding that some type of continued life form—often a mode of personal continuation—exists after the death of the physical body. This has been described as "beliefs in an afterlife," but it may be of many types, such as those involving the soul's ongoing life in heaven without the body or the reincarnation of a soul in a new and different body. Speece and Brent (in press) have labeled this notion "noncorporeal continuation," but even that phrase might be challenged by those who believe in a non-personal continuation or in a resurrection of the body. Researchers have not agreed about some type of continued life form as a subconcept in the master concept of death, even though many children and adults include this element in their understandings of death.

Children's Questions About Death

One way to appreciate children's striving to understand the concept of death and its various subconcepts is to attend to the cognitive efforts that are represented by their questions. What are the challenges confronting children in this endeavor? And what are some questions that children typically employ when they are coping with these challenges?

(1) Universality

(a) **All inclusiveness.** When children try to grasp the universality of death in terms of its "all inclusiveness," they ask themselves and others questions like the following:

- Does *everyone* die?
- Do children or animals die, too?
- Can some people (animals or other living things) *escape* death?
- Could I or the people that I know and love *avoid* coming to be dead?

(b) **Inevitability.** When children try to grasp the "inevitability" of death, they ask themselves and others questions that are closely related to those just mentioned:

- Does everyone *have* to die?
- Do *you* have to die?
- Do *I* have to die?
- Is death something that *must happen* to living things?

These last questions lead some children to wonder about the possibility that death might not be inevitable:

- Could some living things *avoid* death?
- If so, for which things is death not inevitable?
- Can we prevent living things from dying?
- What can I do so that I will never have to die?
- Why does death have to happen?

(c) **Unpredictability.** When children try to understand the "unpredictability" of death, they ask themselves and others questions like the following about the exact timing of death:

- *When* do people or other living things die?
- When will you die?
- When will I die?

In response to such questions, there is a powerful urge to say: *"Not for a very long time."* In many cases, perhaps even in most cases, that may be true. But if death is truly unpredictable, how can we be sure? How can an unpredictable event be known in advance—except in its all inclusive universality and inevitability? How can death be both absolutely necessary and yet uncertain or unpredictable?

A child who pursues reflections on the theme of unpredictability in the subconcept of death's universality, is likely to encounter even harder questions with a powerful personal impact:

- How can it be that we know that death *must* come to all living things without *also* knowing *when* death will or must occur?
- If it is generally true that we do not know in advance precisely when an individual will die, does that mean that *any* living person or thing might die at *any* time?
- Could *you* die at any time?
- Could *I* die at any time?

(2) Irreversibility

Children who are striving to master the subconcept of "irreversibility" ask themselves and others questions like the following:

- *How long* do you stay dead after you die?
- Once you have been "deaded" are you *always* dead?
- Can dead persons *become alive again* after they are dead?
- If I did some special thing (e.g., called 911 or gave someone a pill) to someone who was dead, could he or she be alive again?
- Can you or I come back to life after you or I die?

3) Nonfunctionality

Children who are striving to master the subconcept of "nonfunctionality" ask themselves and others questions like the following:

- *What do you do* all the time when you're dead?
- Can you see anything, hear noises, or feel the heat and the cold when you're dead?

◆ Do dead people continue to eat, play, or go to the bathroom? Do dead people get angry or sad?

(4) Causality

When children strive to grasp the "causality" of death, they ask themselves and others questions like the following:

◆ *Why* do people die?
◆ What caused the death of my pet cat? What is it that *makes* living things die? Do people die because they are bad?
◆ Can people die because someone wished that they would die?
◆ When Mommy was mad at me and said, "You'll be the death of me some day," and then was in the accident, did that mean that I made her die?

(5) Some Type of Continued Life Form

Children who are striving to grasp or to articulate their understanding of some type of continued life form as a part of their overall concept of death, ask themselves and others questions like the following:

◆ What happens *after* death?
◆ *Where* does your *soul* go when you die?
◆ Even though my body dies, will my *spirit* go on to a better life?
◆ Will *I* ever come back to life again?
◆ Will I be alive again *in this body* or *in some different form*?

Comparing Younger Children to Older Children

Adults often inquire about differences between the ways in which younger and older children understand death and its subconcepts. Some general guidelines can be offered on this subject, but the present state of our knowledge suggests caution in claims about what we think we know concerning children's understandings of death and about how we use our knowledge.

As a general rule, younger children in our society are more likely than older children to indicate that death is: not universal, avoidable, or only occurs in the remote future; temporary and reversible in spontaneous, magical, medical, or other ways; a state in which the dead and their bodies continue to engage in various activities; and the result of unrealistic, specific, concrete, or external causes.

Much of this is not surprising. Young children are quite familiar with everyday experiences such as going to sleep (and waking up) or departing (and returning). These are temporary and reversible experiences. Similarly, young children experience many events in their lives in which undesirable outcomes are threatened, only to be avoided in actual fact. News reports tell of seemingly inexplicable (marvelous? magical? miraculous?) escapes from death or startling resuscitations. Also, many fairy tales (e.g., Snow White) and other stories (e.g., "E.T.") describe dead persons as continuing to engage in ongoing activities or as coming back to life in one way or another.

Older children in our society are more likely than their younger counterparts to grasp the key elements that are involved in the sub-concept of the universality of death (its all inclusiveness, inevitability, and puzzling unpredictability), its finality in the twin senses of irreversibility and cessation of bodily functioning, and its authentic causality.

It is not fully clear, for children or for adults, what is involved in a mature understanding of some type of continued life form. Perhaps the task is to determine whether or not one accepts some type of continued life form after death and to integrate that with the rest of one's concept of death?

A Stage-Based Description of Children's Understandings of Death

Differences noted between younger and older children's understandings of the concept of death or of its subconcepts have led some researchers (e.g., Nagy, 1948) to claim that there are fairly clear *"stages"* that can be distinguished in the development of children's understandings of death. A typical account might identify three stages in this process:

1. a first stage in which children do not grasp the finality of death (usually by equating it either with something like travel and ongoing life in another place or with sleep and ongoing life in some diminished form);

2. a second stage in which children do grasp that death is final whenever it does occur, but add the claim that death can be

avoided in some way (e.g., by outwitting death—which is often thought of as an external force); and

3. a third stage in which children grasp that death is both final and not avoidable, i.e., irreversible and universal.

This is a plausible account which brings out some of the central themes noted above in children's understandings of death. It has the special advantage of fitting into much larger theoretical schemas which have proven attractive to many students of cognitive development in childhood. According to these larger schemas, children move from concrete intellectual operations to more abstract or conceptual ways of thinking as they mature. As a broad generalization about cognitive development, this account has many advantages.

However, as a way of describing the development of children's understandings of death there are many pitfalls in both the structure and the application of this stage-based theory.

Typically, this approach isolates cognitive development from other aspects of human maturation. Usually, not much attention is paid to life experiences, individual personality, methodological limitations affecting the research design, or other factors which might bear on a fuller account of what children know about death and why they think about it in these ways.

More importantly, children are not elevators operating in uniform ways in three-level buildings. Development in children is much more complex, variable, and individualized than a stage-based metaphor would suggest. Such development in an individual child is more like that in *a grove of trees;* it has many simultaneous dimensions, processes, and rates, and it is affected by a variety of individual and environmental factors.

Further, both proponents and users of stage-based theories have all too often tended to link claims about *stages in children's cognitive development* to the ages of the children in question. Perhaps some of this is our fault. We have wanted so much to know (without asking them) how children in a certain age group think about death or what they might be capable of thinking about death. The problem is that linking children's understandings of death to their ages confounds a developmental theory with chronological issues. It simply conflicts with our awareness that all children do not develop at the same pace or in the same ways.

A Task-Based Description of Children's Understandings of Death

This account has not stressed the so-called "stages" in children's understandings of death. Instead, we have emphasized a more subtle and complex description of what is involved for children in grasping the concept of death than the version usually given in standard stage-based theories. Each of the five subconcepts or components in the overall concept of death presents its own challenges to children—as their sometimes puzzling questions indicate. Each of these aspects of the concept of death calls upon children to strive to master its constituent meanings and to cope with its implications.

One way to depict this process is to view it as a series of interrelated intellectual *"tasks"* in which children strive to gain an understanding of both the content and the implications of death and its subconcepts. Such task work is taken up and pursued at different times and in diverse situations in the lives of children. Instead of being finished once and for all at specific ages or stages of development, these tasks ordinarily lead to increased insight, appreciation, and complexity throughout a child's life. With richer understandings of death, children can forge enhanced links between the concept of death, its subconcepts, and their other ideas. And as their understandings of death (and life) become more subtle, the mental worlds of children equip them to cope more effectively with their experiences and concerns.

A task-based account of children's understandings of death moves away from *two pitfalls* that often afflict stage-based theories and their use:

1. stereotypical descriptions and sequencing of the "stages" in what children are thought to know about death; and
2. potentially misleading linkages between chronological age and cognitive development.

In avoiding these pitfalls, a task-based account of children's understandings of death challenges adults who want to appreciate these understandings to do at least three things:

1. listen actively to each child with whom they come into contact in order to learn what that particular child does or does not understand about death;

2. inquire as to the precise focus of the conceptual task(s) with which that child is struggling; and
3. let the child tell us what he or she does or does not now understand about death.

As we enter into the world of children's understandings of death, adults are also challenged to reflect on how we ourselves have coped with the subconcepts of universality, irreversibility, nonfunctionality, causality, and some type of continued life form in our own understandings of death. And we may appreciate that success in these tasks is more like a long-term project, perhaps a lifelong endeavor, in which one comes to realize (or "make real" in his or her inner psychic world) in both sudden, unexpected ways and in slower, more gradual ways what he or she thinks about the concept of death and about the meaning or relevance of that many-hued concept for his or her life.

Children Who are Coping with Loss, Grief, or Life-Threatening Illness

Children who are engaged in the difficult intellectual work of trying to understand the concept of death may also be *children who are coping with loss, grief, or life-threatening illness.* If so, the cognitive task work that we have been describing here may be linked to other tasks that define such coping work. Recently, coping with loss, grief, and life-threatening illness has been described in terms of several task-based models (Corr & Doka, 1994).

For example, Fox (1988) described children's tasks in coping with loss and grief as ways to insure that their "grief work" is in fact "good grief." With some modifications, Fox's four tasks are:

1. to understand and begin to make sense out of what has happened;
2. to identify, validate, and express in constructive ways strong reactions to the loss;
3. to commemorate the life that was lived; and
4. to learn to go on with living and loving.

Much of this depends on an individual child's understanding of death, its various subconcepts, the specific circumstances of his or her loss, and what all this means for his or her life.

Similarly, Doka (1993) identified tasks that are involved in living with life-threatening illness. Doka described different tasks at different points in the illness trajectory:

1. prior to diagnosis—for example, in recognizing possible danger or risk;
2. at the time of diagnosis—for example, in understanding the disease and developing strategies to deal with the issues it presents;
3. during the chronic phase of the illness—for example, in managing stress and preserving self concept;
4. in the experience of recovery (if that should occur)—for example, in dealing with aftereffects of illness or fears of recurrence;
5. in the terminal phase of illness--for example, in preparing for death, saying good-bye, and finding meaning in life and death.

For children, the point is that all of these tasks in coping with life-threatening illness depend at least in part upon their understandings of loss and death, the implications of those understandings, and the responses that arise from such understandings.

Conclusion

When a significant person in a child's life is dying or has died, it is not surprising to hear questions like the following:

◆   Why did it happen?
◆   Did I cause it?
◆   Will it happen to me?
◆   When will the person be back?
◆   Who will take care of me?

These are powerful questions which are closely interwoven with understandings of life-threatening illness, death, and its consequences. Responses to such questions must be informed, supportive, and sensitive to the needs of the particular child.

Even when illness and loss are not critical matters for a specific child, death can be a puzzling part of life. In short, children can and will encounter death-related issues and concerns throughout their lives.

Whenever children have such encounters, it is important for them to feel free to ask questions about death and its significance.

Questions concerning physical, psychological, social, and spiritual implications of death can aid children in their own development, enable adults to help children, and enrich adult understandings of death.

In response to a child's questions about death, adults can share insights, experiences, and ways of interpreting what he or she needs to know. To do so, as Carl Jung (1954, p. 7) once wrote, "we need certain points of view for their orienting and heuristic value; but they should always be regarded as mere auxiliary concepts that can be laid aside at any time." The main thing is to listen actively to children, to respond to their questions as best we can, and to share with them as rich a life as death and other factors make possible.

References

Brent, S. B., & Speece, M. W. (1993). "Adult" conceptualization of irreversibility: Implications for the development of the concept of death. *Death Studies*, 17, 203-224.

Corr, C. A., & Doka, K. J. (1994). Current models of death, dying, and bereavement. *Critical Care Nursing Clinics of North America*, 6(3), 545-552.

Doka, K. J. (1993). *Living with life-threatening illness*. Lexington, MA: Lexington Books.

Fox, S. S. (1988). *Good grief: Helping groups of children when a friend dies*. Boston: The New England Association for the Education of Young Children.

Jung, C. G. (1954). *The development of personality*. In J. Read, M. Fordham, & G. Adler (Eds.), *The collected works of C. G. Jung*, Vol. 17. New York: Pantheon Books, Random House.

Nagy, M. A. (1948). The child's theories concerning death. *Journal of Genetic Psychology*, 73, 3-27.

Speece, M. W., & Brent, S. B. (in press). The development of children's understanding of death. In C. A. Corr & D. M. Corr (Eds.), *Helping children cope with death and bereavement*. New York: Springer Publishing Co.

Grieving Children: Can We Answer Their Questions? 2

Rabbi Earl A. Grollman

It was three decades ago when I wrote my book *Explaining Death to Children*. At that time it was a taboo subject. Somehow many people believed that if death were not discussed, it would magically disappear.

Since that time we have learned that just as we cannot protect ourselves from life, so we cannot protect our youngsters from death. Traumatic experiences belong to both adulthood and childhood.

Where can one turn in tragedy if no one will admit that there is a tragedy? If loss can be acknowledged, we find comfort in what we can mean to each other—even in the midst of lingering pain and loneliness.

Death is a universal and inevitable process that must be faced by people of all ages. Children who are able to participate with adults after the death of someone they love will be better equipped to understand and manage the emotions of their grief. It is in this spirit that I share with you many of the questions that are asked by adults and children when a loved one has died.

Shouldn't Children Be Shielded From Death?

Death is a crisis which should be shared by *all members of the family.* Children are too often forgotten by grieving adults. Silence and secrecy deprive them of an important opportunity to share grief. When, in our understandable heartache, we overlook their feelings, we heighten their sense of isolation. Reality is replaced with psychological defenses. Now, the youngsters need our help to sort out their emotions. When we discuss death with our children openly, we enable them to live more freely.

Too often feelings and perspectives of youngsters are overlooked because of the false assumption that young people are just too sensitive and cannot possibly cope with this difficult subject. Yet, in reality they are confronted with it in word and song, in the natural world of plants and animals, as well as among their families and friends, and in the daily news when a space shuttle explodes before their very eyes.

Good mental health is not the denial of tragedy, but the frank acknowledgment of painful separation. One of the worst difficulties is youngsters' lack of understanding because of adult secrecy. Remember—a person is a person, no matter how small.

But If Adults Are Confused, Then How Can They Help Children?

It is true adults do not understand the complete meaning of death. And professionals continue to wrestle with this thorny question as well. No mortal has ever pierced the veil of its great mystery. Yet, we have the inescapable responsibility to share with our children the fragments of our experience and knowledge.

While insight is a gift, we must first place ourselves in a position to receive it. Children should be encouraged to tell *us* how *they* feel about death, what *they* think, what *they* know, where *they* need to go. We should respond by trying to let them know that we understand what they are trying to say. We should attempt to answer the question in the spirit in which it is asked.

Do not teach children as if we have the final answers that they must accept. We show our maturity when we respond: "Are you surprised that I do not know everything about death? Don't be. Yet we can still talk about it. You can learn something from me. I can learn something from you. We can help each other."

How Do I Begin To Explain Death?

Do not start by asking, "Have you ever thought what you will do when I die?" Such an introduction is security-shaking for both adult and child. Nor should the initial explanation be based on dogma, belief, or theology. Philosophical interpretations are too abstract for a child to comprehend.

Death and its meaning should be approached gently, indirectly, tenderly. An explanation might involve trees and leaves and how long they last. Point out the diverse forms, shapes, and colors of nature, such as bugs, snails, butterflies. Once they moved; now are quietly still. Start with non-threatening examples and proceed slowly, step by step, in accordance with the child's ability to understand.

Can Children Really Understand Death?

What should we tell children about the words DIE and DEAD? Our answers should correspond to the developmental age of our youngsters, the nature of the death, and their emotional involvement with it. Even children of the same age differ widely in their behavior and development: some are mature and stable even when faced with tragedy; others are seemingly immature and may seem younger in relation to their years. Remember that appearances can be deceiving. The child who seems to be the most "collected" may be most upset inside.

Do not try to fit your youngster's perception of death into a fixed age category. For every child, the meaning of death is reexamined as life changes. The concept of death undergoes a continuous process of maturation. The following guidelines should be viewed as only general approximations:

Very young children believe in magic. All things are possible and believable. Stones can talk, princes turn into frogs and back into princes. The beautiful princess, asleep for 100 years, is awakened by a kiss from the handsome prince. To pre-schoolers, death is reversible. If we go on a trip, we come back. Perhaps death is a long trip from which the loved one *will* return. For the young child, living "infinity years" may seem possible and realistic.

Between the ages of 5 and 9, children are better able to understand the meaning of physical death because of their developing life experiences. They start to worry about the non-existence of people close to them. They may conceive of death as a bogeyman, a ghost, an angel of death, dressed in white or black who comes to take people away.

By the time children are 9 or 10, and thereafter, they formulate more realistic concepts based on biological observations and wider experience. Death may no longer be embodied in human or supernatural form. Death is an end of bodily life. It is final and universal.

Dr. Robert Kastenbaum of the Arizona State University tells us that adolescents and even adults have childlike views of death. They "know" that death is inevitable and final, but most of their daily attitudes and actions are more consistent with the conviction that personal death is an unfounded rumor.

How Do We Tell Children About The Death?

It is important that youngsters be informed *immediately*. If possible, they should be told by a parent or someone close to them. It is advisable to relay the sad news in familiar surroundings, preferably at home. Delay makes it all the more possible that children will be told of the death by the wrong person, at the wrong place, and in the wrong way.

There is no "right" or "proper" way. *What* is said is significant, but how it is said will have a greater bearing on whether youngsters develop unnecessary fears or will be able to accept, within their abilities, the reality of death. Approach the child gently and with love. The tone of voice—warm, sympathetic, and kind—will communicate feelings more completely than any specific words.

Stay close to the children, hug them, and let them feel your warmth and affection. Proceed gradually, according to their intellectual and emotional capabilities. Speak simply and accurately; be consistent in what you say. Don't overwhelm them with too much detail. Again, concepts about death should be translated into the language and comprehension level of the youngsters. Try to avoid theological abstractions. Never link death with sin and divine punishment. Children experience enough guilt without an added measure of chastisement.

Children need to talk, not just to be talked to. Ask them if they have any questions. Try to hear not only their words but their nonverbal communication as well. Allow them to reveal their fears and anxieties. Do not misinterpret natural curiosity as morbid or bizarre.

Don't be surprised if, after we have informed them of the death, they ask to go out and play, or change the subject entirely. What we may consider indifference, simply represents the limits of a child's ability to cope with loss. The fact of death may be so disturbing and so frightening that the child cannot handle it all at once. It is a way of saying, "I just can't believe it."

What Are Some Responses That Children May Have?

For the child, death may bring a variety of reactions:

Denial: "I don't believe it. It didn't happen. It is just a dream. Daddy will come back. He will! He will!"

The child may frequently look as if she were unaffected because she is trying to defend herself against the death by pretending that it had not really happened. We may even feel that the child's apparent unconcern is heartless. Or we may be relieved and feel, "Isn't it lucky! I am sure she misses her parent, but she does not seem to be really bothered by it." Usually the lack of response signifies that the child has found the loss too great to accept and goes on pretending secretly that the person is still alive.

Bodily Distress: "I have a tightness in my throat." "I can't breath." "I have no appetite at all." "I have no strength." "I am exhausted." "I can't do my homework." "I can't sleep." "I had a nightmare." "I don't feel well enough to go to school."

The anxiety has expressed itself in physical and emotional symptoms.

Hostile Reactions to the Deceased: "How could Daddy do this to me?" "Didn't he care enough for me to stay alive?" "Why did he leave me?" The child feels deserted, abandoned and angry.

Hostile Reactions to Others: "It's the doctor's fault. She gave him the wrong medicine." Or, "Mother didn't take proper care of him. That's why he died."

The resentment is projected outward in order to relieve guilt by making someone else responsible for the death.

Idealization: "How dare you say anything against Daddy! He was perfect."

In the attempt to fight off his or her own unhappy thoughts, the child becomes obsessed with the father's good qualities. The falsification is out of keeping with the father's real life and character.

Panic: "Who will take care of me now?" "Suppose something happens to Mommy?" "Daddy used to bring home money for food and toys. Who will get these things for us?"

This state of confusion and shock needs the adult's supportive love: "My health is fine. I will take care of you. There is enough money for food and toys."

Guilt: Children are very likely to feel guilt since, in their experience, bad things happen to them because they were naughty. The desertion of the loved one "must" be a retribution for their wrong-doing. Therefore, they search their minds for the "bad deed" that caused it.

Many young children harbor fantasies that they are responsible for the death in the family. They often believe in a primitive magic. That is, if one wishes someone harm, the belief will bring results. The boy said to his sister: "I wish you were dead." Then when the sibling died a year later, the lad was terror stricken by his own powers. Or the child may fear that he made his mother work too hard. He can still recall her saying: "You're such a messy kid. Picking up after you will be the death of me yet." This is why it is so necessary to help the child express his or her own fantasies and fears.

Are Fairy Tales A Helpful Explanation For The Enigma Of Death?

The question arises constantly about what we should tell a child when death occurs. Should we avoid acknowledgment that the person has died? Should we suggest that a grandfather became ill and had to go away to a hospital where he could recuperate and become cured, hoping that his memory would gradually fade away and the youngster would come to accept the absence as being the norm?

Evasions indicate the uncertainty which the adult has about the child's capacity to deal with existing situations. It encourages the youngster to develop the capacity to "forget about things" and does not prepare him or her to deal with life's realities. We should never cover up with a fiction which we will some day repudiate. There is no greater child need than trust and truth.

Use words like "die" or "dead"; *not* "went away on a long journey," "left," "lost," or "passed away." Distortions of reality create lasting harm. It is far healthier to share the quest for wisdom than to appease immediate curiosity with fairy tales in the guise of fact.

How About Explaining An Afterlife To Children?

The concept of heaven is difficult for a child to grasp. "But Daddy, if Mommy is going to heaven, then why are they putting her in the ground?" Some children peer from an airplane window seeking the loved one. Others hope rain coming down from heaven will bring the loved one back to earth.

We may feel that our own beliefs are too stark for a youngster—that it would be more comforting to express a religious conviction that we do not personally hold. So we spin out a tale of heavenly happiness while hopeless finality fills our own heart. We comfort the child by saying, "Mommy will always be with us," while we mourn that person as irretrievably gone. Children have built-in radar and quickly detect inconsistency and deception. Share honest religious convictions, but be prepared for further questions concerning simplistic theological terms. Religious convictions *can* bring comfort and understanding to children if they are carefully explained.

Do not, however, paint too beautiful a picture of the world-to-come. Some children have attempted suicide in the hope of joining the absent loved one. By taking their own lives, they intend to restore the loss and at the same time be with God in Paradise.

You and your children may wish to discuss the thoughts of an afterlife with a clergy person.

Should The Child Be Discouraged From Crying?

Only the insensitive person could say of a child who had encountered tragedy and remained dispassionate: "The child is taking it so well. She never cries."

Crying is a natural emotion. A newborn enters life crying for more oxygen. In early life, tears are an infant's means of expressing needs, pains, and discomforts. Even after children are able to verbalize their desires, they continue to weep in order to release painful emotion. Weeping helps to express that inevitable depth of despair that follows the slow realization that the death is not a bad dream.

Do not feel as if we have failed when we weep in front of our child. The opposite is true, for it expresses the undeniable fact that we too are human and need emotional release. It is better to say, "I could cry, too," rather than, "There, you mustn't cry." For tears are wordless messages, a vital part of grieving for people of all ages.

Should The Child Attend The Funeral?

The funeral is a rite of passage, an important occasion in the life of the family. The bad dream is real. The beloved will no longer be a part of the familiar environment. Like other members of the household, children should have the privilege of expressing their love and devotion.

Participation aids children in understanding the finality of death and in dispelling the fantasies of young, fertile imaginations. If they are old enough to attend a service and comprehend in part what is taking place, they should be allowed to attend a ceremony to say farewell to a significant person in their lives.

Many children are discomfited by their unfamiliarity with the funeral rites and setting. Explain in advance approximately how the chapel will look and where they will be sitting. If unable to be close to them at the service, ask a member of the family or a friend to be with them and perhaps to hold their hand.

No matter how helpful and therapeutic the funeral may be— children should not be *forced* to attend. If apprehensive youngsters elect to remain at home, don't place any "shaming" pressures upon them or insinuate that they may not have loved the person who died. Gently suggest that together we might visit the cemetery at another time.

What About Going To The Cemetery?

The funeral does not end in the chapel, but after the dead person has been accompanied to the final burial place. Don't assume arbitrarily that the interment is too traumatic for children. Again, explain in detail the procedure, and consult them about their wishes and needs. Witnessing the burial may provide a realistic answer to the perennial question: "Where is my loved one now?"

How About After The Funeral?

Just as children cannot be protected from the reality of death, so they cannot and should not be excluded from the grief and mourning following the burial.

Immediately notify the child's school or day care center about the death. Often children regress, do less well, or seem "out-of-it."

Inform the school so that teachers may understand the child's possible changing behavior. Staff can offer extra support and understanding only when notified of the crisis in the child's life.

Also consider death education as part of school curriculum. Clifton Fadiman wrote in the afterword of Louisa May Alcott's *Little Men:* "The most moving episode has to do with John Brooke's death and funeral. As I read it, I found myself wondering why most books for children these days are afraid to mention death." It's not a question of whether children will receive death education, since they witness so much violence on television. The challenge is to provide death education which is helpful and informative.

Do not change the role of the child. The living youngster does not replace a dead sibling. When a parent dies, the child does not suddenly become the "man" or "woman" of the house. Children should be encouraged to be with their own friends and become reinvolved with their usual activities. No child (or adult) should be told to "be brave." Having to put up a false front makes grieving that much more difficult.

Consider a grief support system. Youngsters may wish to join a group of others who are grieving. Learning about the experiences of peers may offer invaluable insights into their own feelings. Many times children have difficulty in speaking to significant adults. They say:

> "I was afraid to cry in front of my parents because I didn't want to upset them anymore than they were."

> "People always ask how my parents are doing, but never ask how I am."

> "I thought I should be over my pain after the first week."

After attending peer support groups, they reported:

> "I understand now that I'm not alone."

> "My feelings are okay."

> "It helped to know that I'm not crazy."

> *"I could hear others say things that I was afraid to admit."*
Children need support, encouragement and friendship just as do adults.

We might wish to make referrals to supportive professionals. For the question is not *how* is the child acting, reacting, or overreacting but for *how long.* After an initial period of mourning, children are often able to work themselves back to some degree of productive and near-normal living. After several months have elapsed, danger signals may be present if the children continue to:

◆ look sad all the time and experience prolonged depression
◆ keep up a hectic pace and cannot relax the way they used to with you and their friends
◆ not care about how they dress and look
◆ seem tired, or unable to sleep, with their health suffering markedly
◆ avoid social activities and wish to be alone more and more
◆ be indifferent to school and hobbies they once enjoyed
◆ experience feelings of worthlessness and self-incrimination
◆ rely on drugs and/or alcohol
◆ let their moods control them instead of controlling their moods.

If there are doubts, do not hesitate to seek advice from a therapist, psychiatrist, psychologist, or child guidance clinic. There are times when even the best-informed and well-intentioned adults are simply inadequate. Getting professional assistance is not an admission of weakness but a demonstration of real love and strength.

Most important we must give *continued* assurance of love and support. The greatest gift we can bring to our children is ourselves. Our caring and concern over the next months and years will be of inestimable value in aiding recovery. Be willing to *listen* for minutes, hours, days. Youngsters need to talk, not just be talked to. Many children have an almost insatiable need to pour out their feelings.

Try to recall the wonderfully happy times shared together, not just the sad moment of death. Youngsters should be reminded that the loss of one important relationship does not necessarily mean the loss of others—including the one with you.

When words fail, touch! Attitude can be more important than words. Physical demonstrations of love and support are the greatest gift to a grieving child. As we adults walk the long and difficult path of separation, we may find with our children new dimensions in the capacity for caring and understanding. In truth, for people of all ages . . .

healing is a process, recovery is a choice!

A Final Thought

Talking about death is often a complex and disturbing task. In the end, of course what we feel will determine what we teach our children. If adults are disturbed by the thought of death, the child will feel their anxieties and tensions too. Regardless of language employed, emotional tones are transmitted.

The denial of death can lead us to the edge of the abyss and threaten our existence with meaninglessness and futility; acceptance will help us and our children start to build a bridge to span that chasm with the things of life that still count—memory, family, friendship, love. Most important for us and our children is the knowledge that life continues despite pain. Grief is a strange mixture of joy and sorrow—joy to be alive and sorrow to have life diminished by the loss of the one you love.

◆

Section Two

The Child's Response To Life-Threatening Illness

Children not only face death in general terms. Many times, their experience of death takes place in intensely personal ways. In some cases they may be coping with the loss of someone significant in their own life. In other cases, it is their own life-threatening illness that causes a confrontation with the specter of death.

In the first chapter in this section, Doka offers general guidelines for talking to children about illness. Whether it's their own or someone else's. Doka makes two critical points. First, despite an inclination toward protecting the child from troubling information, it is essential that the child both be informed or involved in the illness. Second, Doka suggests that communication to the child be framed by three questions: What does the child want to know? What does the child need to know? What can the child understand?

Alexander also emphasizes some of these same themes as he reviews the difficulties that children and their families face as they cope with life-threatening illness. Alexander stresses that while children have to deal with special issues in a life-threatening illness, the ways they deal with them will be affected by their own developmental levels. Alexander also reaffirms the need for open communication between the family and child. Finally, he reminds us that hospice care can provide essential support in the terminal phase. In the words of Dr. Patricia Murphy, "Hospice care is not the admis-

here is nothing more to do. Rather, it is aggressive comfort that works hard to maintain a quality of life until it ends."

Anderson's chapter contributes still another understanding. Anderson explores the crisis posed by the epidemic of AIDS. Anderson's chapter emphasizes how much the experience of life-threatening illness is influenced both by the disease itself as well as social variables such as class and culture. Anderson makes one additional point clearly evident in AIDS but true in every other illness as well. Far more people are affected by disease than infected by it.

Taken together, these three chapters reaffirm Alexander's conclusion, "Be Loving. Be Supportive. Be There. The child will need you."

Talking to Children about Illness

3

Kenneth J. Doka

Introduction

A number of years ago Robert Kastenbaum (1973) wrote a fascinating article entitled "The Kingdom Where Nobody Dies." Kastenbaum's point was that we often try to protect children from death and illness yet, as Kastenbaum indicates, children are well aware of both.

Certainly T.V. abounds with images of illness and death. Themes of illness, loss, and death are also evident in fairy tales, children's stories, jokes, songs, even games. One theory of the origin of "ring-around-the rosie" sees it as a chant to ward off the bubonic plague.

We do try to protect children from illness and death. We see illness and death as one of the many harsh realities that we do not wish to see intrude on the child's world. So when we cannot avoid these discussions, we often try to discuss it with romantic images or euphemistic terms, often confusing children.

Trying to protect children from illness and loss is understandable. It can be difficult to discuss these issues. We feel it is hard for children to understand. It is certainly hard for us to explain.

Yet these attempts to protect children from illness and death are often futile. First, children can have a tremendous amount of medical sophistication. Especially by middle childhood, they have studied diseases, perhaps had experiences with the illness of others, and have certainly seen images in the media.

When the illness involves them personally, either their own or someone in their family or circle, they often have external cues. They can sense the anxieties and concerns around them. They know that conversations cease when they enter a room. They see friends and relatives visiting from distant places. One boy with leukemia told me he learned of the seriousness of his illness when he casually mentioned to his mother that he would like to be a fireman one day.

His mother hugged him tightly, fearfully telling him he would. The ten-year-old wryly remarked "I never knew she cared so much about firemen."

When the illness is the child's, the child also has three additional sources of information. First, children respond to their own internal cues. They know they are in pain, they can sense when they are weaker and sicker. Second, if they are in a hospital or outpatient clinic they can often guess what types of patients are treated. Third, often their peers are effective sources of information. Bluebond-Langner (1978) in her study of children with life-threatening illness, pointed out that these children were well aware of their condition even when parents and staff consciously sought to withhold information.

Keeping information from a child is not only futile; it is also harmful. It inhibits the child from seeking support, creates additional anxiety, impairs trust and complicates the child's response to a crisis. For example, one eight-year-old was convinced that his parents lied to him about his mother's initial hospitalization. When his father finally told him of his mother's illness he had to work through his anger before he could even respond to his mother's needs.

The goal of this paper is to discuss how to talk about life-threatening or serious illness with a child, whether that illness is the child's own or another's. The paper begins by addressing the communicative context that frames any discussion. It then offers guidelines that should help adults in addressing the child's needs and concerns.

The Communicative Context

There are three questions that should be considered before discussing an illness with a child. They are: What does a child need to know? What does a child want to know? What can a child understand?

Whenever an illness intrudes upon a child's world, whether it is the child's illness or another in the child's circle, there is information that should be shared with the child. First, the child should understand what, in fact, is wrong. If someone in the child's family is ill, it is important that the child be aware of the situation. In many cases, the child will recognize that others in the family are concerned and troubled by something. If the child is left uninformed he or she may imagine all sorts of things that might account for the observed change. In one family, for example, a child's mother was to undergo a biopsy for a growth. The young girl sensed the concern. She was quietly convinced that her parents were about to divorce.

Sometimes children may even blame themselves for the concerns, anxieties and behavioral changes they sense around them. Knowing that there is a concern not only relieves them of the anxiety, but allows them to offer support.

Even if the knowledge could be successfully withheld from the child, it would not be helpful to do so. Should the illness proceed, the child may feel left out or distrustful since he/she did not know earlier or missed opportunities to participate in care. If the ill person dies, the lack of knowledge about prior illness may make the death that much more shocking. A friend once shared her reactions to her grandmother's death. She was 10 years old when her grandmother, who lived in Florida, became ill with cancer. Though they were separated, they corresponded regularly and the granddaughter visited twice a year, during winter and summer vacations. Her parents withheld information about the illness. Her grandmother deteriorated rather rapidly. When she died, my friend was surprised since she had seen her grandmother three months ago and was unaware of her illness. She also felt robbed of any opportunity to share her love with her grandmother.

When the illness affects the child personally, the child also needs to know what is occurring. Naturally (as will be addressed later in this chapter) this may be done differently at different ages. For example, a young child who is HIV positive may need to know he/she has a blood disease that requires him/her to take medicine and special care. An older child may need more explicit information.

Related to the question "what is wrong?" is the question "how does it affect me?" Children, like most of us, always want to know the personal implications. If the child is ill, the disease may affect them in a number of ways. They may need to participate in treatment. The illness may curtail activities. While one may not want to discuss *potential* long-term implications, it is worth while to at least discuss the immediate and short-term effects of the illness. For only if the child understands these effects can the child become an active participant in the treatment. Becoming a partner in treatment is one of the best ways to assist adherence to a medical regimen.

Even if another is ill, the child is likely to be affected. There may be less time available for the child, or less money. Parents may be anxious or out of town. The child may have to take on additional responsibilities, perhaps curtail activities. Again honest discussions with a child may help adults and children solve problems and plan in partnership easing future anger and resentments.

I remember when I was about 10 years old, my mother became ill for a period of time. I felt proud that I was included in family conferences. Understanding my mother's illness probably made me less demanding and more conscious of the ways I could help and assist. I felt part of a family.

A third question the child needs to know is "what can be done?" Explaining the actions that can be taken can restore a sense of control in what may be a frightening time. It is important though to be honest. Blindly assuring the child that everything will be all right may not be realistic and later may make the child distrustful. Honest and hopeful responses such as "we are doing all we can" are both truthful and reassuring.

In addition to what a child needs to know, adults have to be sensitive to what a child wants to know. It is important to recognize that the child's questions are good indicators of what the child is ready to hear. Adults though should clarify a child's questions. "Is mommy going to die?" can be a request for information, reassurance or both. Talking about the question as well as the answer, rather than simply and unequivocally responding are the best ways to understand the child's concerns and keep open lines of communication.

Listen for any underlying sensitivities. Many questions may be subtly asking "am I to blame?" Children, especially younger children, may exhibit magical thinking, not always drawing clearly cause and effects. In addition, guilt is a common coping response to any crisis. Children may feel that their own thoughts or behaviors may have brought the illness on themselves or others.

In one case, a five year old girl with leukemia began to tell me a story of her mother's dog who was run over by a car. Some careless person, she related, had left the gate open. Surely that person would be punished she asked. As we discussed this, she revealed that she was that careless person. Her illness, she reasoned, was God's way of punishing her. Only by sensitively responding to the underlying question of blame, could the child find the reassurance she needed.

A final question is "what can the child understand?" Adults need to recognize that children are on different developmental levels. At different ages their vocabulary, sense of cause and effect, presence of magical thinking, and ability to understand abstract thought differ. Their experiences may differ as well. It is easier to explain an illness to someone who has had experience with illness, even another's, than one whose experience is more limited.

There may be other considerations that can affect understanding. Children who have developmental disabilities or learning difficulties may find it more difficult to understand illness. Other considerations too may play a role. For example the tremendous fear that AIDS or HIV infection generates can inhibit understanding. It may affect communication in other ways. One child with sickle-cell anemia when told he had a blood disease, immediately assumed it was AIDS, given the community epidemic and the fact that it too is a disease associated with blood. Understanding the communicative context requires not only a comprehension of what, but also when and how. Illness should be explained in a calm context where the child has opportunity to reflect and question. Remember too that actions such as voice and tone and nonverbal communications such as eye contact, touch and hugs convey as much as what is being said..

Guidelines for Communication

In talking with children about illness, this chapter has affirmed the importance of openness and honesty. Certain principles have been suggested as guidelines for communicating information about illness.

1. Begin on The Child's Level
Children process information differently at varied ages. Younger children tend to be much more concrete while older children are usually capable of some degree of abstract thought. Younger children also tend to be more self-centered, constantly trying to understand information through the prism of self.

It is important then to gear information to the child's own developmental level. Vocabulary and concepts have to be consistent with the child's.

Often it is helpful to begin with the child's experiences. "You know grandma has been ill." "For the past few weeks you have told us how tired you are." Beginning with the child's experience allows one to gear information to the child's own level.

2. Let The Child's Questions Guide.

Adults can often say too much, overwhelming the child with information. It is usually better to begin a dialogue with some basic information and then let the child's questions direct the conversation. Often these questions will tell what the child is able to understand and willing to hear.

As stated earlier, it is important to understand what the child is really asking. It is critical to recognize that children's questions often involve cognitive and and affective dimensions. We need to address both the question and the underlying feeling. I find helpful to use the child's questions as an opening to a dialogue, sometimes asking for further clarification of the question ("are you worried that she is not doing well since your last visit?"), other times offering honest reassurance ("I hope so, but we are not sure right now"), validating feelings ("It's scary that mom's sick"). The point is that the response should be open ended enough to allow the child to address all concerns and questions.

3. Provide Opportunities For The Child To Express Feelings.

Honest communication also means respecting the child's feelings and providing opportunities to openly express those feelings. A child's feelings during illness, whether the child's own or another, can be complex and frightening. Children's feelings may run the gamut of emotions including sadness, anger, guilt, ambivalence, or anxiety.

It is important that the child have opportunities to comfortably express those feelings. Telling a child that they need not feel angry or guilty, or otherwise discounting emotions neither allows further communication nor helps. It is better that the child express those feelings with adults. Adults can help by listening, validating those feelings and sharing their own feelings and the ways that they cope with them.

4. Share Faith.

Our faiths, whether expressed in religious beliefs or philosophical reflections, help us face and transcend crises such as illness and loss. It is often helpful modeling to the child to show the child the ways that one's faith helps one cope with the crisis.

But again, for this to be helpful, these reflections should not be pronouncements that end dialogue and add to the child's burden.

"We must trust God's will and believe" offers a rigidity that children are not likely to find useful in constructing a response to the crisis. On the other hand a comment like "it is so hard to understand why this is happening" allows one to share one's own faith struggle and reaffirm that one's faith helps one cope even when there are no easy answers or explanations. If one does not have an appropriate role to share one's own faith with the child, one can still help the child to reflect upon the ways his or her own beliefs can help as well as to identify with the child sources of support that can seek to further explore concerns.

5. **Encourage Feedback.**

Talking with a child is almost like speaking in a foreign language. One is never quite sure how one's words will be understood especially in anxiety filled crises.

For that reason, it is critical to ask the children to summarize what they have heard. This provides additional opportunities to clarify misunderstandings.

6. **Utilize Other Resources.**

There are many resources that can encourage dialogue. Books and films can often be shared experiences that can facilitate conversation.

There may be other, personal resources. Counselors and peer self-help groups can be very helpful, sometimes permitting children to respond in ways that may not be comfortable with parents. There may also be other adults in the child's world who can be useful sources of support. Whenever I counseled with children I always ask them to name the people with whom they feel comfortable enough to discuss their problems. Helping a child to identify such people reminds them that they need not cope alone.

7. **Use The Child's Natural Expressive Means To Stimulate Dialogue.**

Children often express themselves in stories, games, play, art, or music. Using these approaches with children can be extremely helpful since they are more comfortable to the child, offer direct opportunities for expressing feelings, and provide opportunities for dialogue. Explaining medical procedures with a doll or G.I. Joe figure, talking through a game of "operation" all provide ways to address a child's concerns. Again the approach that one uses should be suited and comfortable to each particular child.

8. Visits and Medical Procedures.

One of the most common questions when someone in the child's family is ill is the question of whether or not the child should visit. I believe that such decisions should be left to the child.

In order to make such a decision, the child will need information, options and support. Fully inform the child what the visit to the hospital will be like. Explain how the person feels, looks and responds. If they are connected to I.V.'s or machines this should be described as well. If they are not in a private room, you may briefly indicate the condition of roommates. This description can provide opportunities to further address the child's concerns.

It is also important to provide options to the child. If they are to have a choice there should be honest alternatives. Staying alone may not be a real alternative, prompting a decision to go even when child is not fully comfortable. It would be better if the child's choice includes an alternative such as staying with an adult they know and trust. If they go to the hospital, children should also know they have choices that will be respected, such as how long they will stay and how close they get. If they decide not to go, there are other options to show their support such as sending letters, tapes, or drawings and calling on the telephone.

A final issue is support. If the child visits there should be one adult whose role is to support the child. This way if the child needs to talk or leave the room that adult can be there to meet the child's needs.

These principles can be adapted if it is the child who is to undergo a medical procedure or hospital visit. Preceding the visit or procedure the child should be informed, in an appropriate manner, of what may be experienced. The child should have an opportunity to share any fears and ask any questions. While the child may not have the opportunity to decide whether or not to have the procedure or enter a hospital, other choices may make it more palatable. For example, the child may choose what to bring, who accompanies, or perhaps, within constraints, time. And naturally throughout this time the child will need the presence of supportive and caring adults.

As one reviews this paper, it may seem that the principles and guidelines offered are useful for a wide variety of contexts. It should not be surprising. After all, the basic theme of this paper is that in illness and loss it is essential to provide the child with opportunities to discuss concerns and address feelings. Honest and direct communication are critical if that is to occur.

There is another moral as well. The commonalty of the principles offered here to other situations reaffirm a basic point. Though one may romanticize childhood, illness and loss are simply other crises that children sometimes must confront.

References

Bluebond-Langner, Myra
1978 *The Private Worlds of Dying Children.* Princeton, N.J. Princeton University Press.

Kastenbaum, Robert
1973 "The Kingdom Where Nobody Dies." *Saturday Review,* January, 33-38.

The Child and Life-Threatening Illness

4

Paul Alexander

Introduction

Children are not supposed to die. They are our eyes, our ears, our hopes and dreams for the future. They remind us of our own innocent times when each birthday brought the ability to do more, to learn more, to venture out further into the world. Just as the thought of facing death provokes anxiety for many adults, the thought of children struggling with life-threatening and terminal illness is even more disturbing. There is no reason for it; we are left feeling helpless and inadequate. It is this unsettling aspect of death's impact that has left many children isolated and lonely during a time of desperate need. An understanding of how children cope with life-threatening illness will enable caregivers to better serve a child, during this crisis time.

This chapter will explore the ways children adjust and integrate, live and die with life-threatening illnesses. In addition, the issue of hospice as a concept of care for a dying child will be addressed.

Life-Threatening Illness: Stages, Phases and Tasks

Life-threatening illness affects children in many ways. They are faced with the threat of the unknown and thrown into a world dominated by medical protocols, varied team of professionals, often painful procedures, schedule changes and uncertainty.

The child's routine world is shattered by a loss of control not only in how the disease affects his or her body, mind and spirit, but also how it influences a once secure world of family, friends, and free time. As we look into the world of children with life-threatening illness we perhaps gain some sense of control and understanding by using theoretical models that categorize it into phases, stages and tasks. The unthinkable becomes somewhat more predictable.

Even as we seek an understanding by observing how children have reacted in similar situations, it is crucial to remember that each child is unique and will face this crisis in his or her own way.

Myra Bluebond-Langner in *The Private Worlds of Dying Children* investigates the stages leukemic children face in the progression of the disease. To Bluebond-Langner, the child understands illness through a complex process of stages.

Stage 1: "It" is a serious illness. Not all children know the name of the illness yet realize something is not right.

Stage 2: The names of the drugs and their side effects are known.

Stage 3: The purpose of the treatment procedures are understood and each procedure and treatment is a unique event.

Stage 4: The disease is seen as a series of relapses and remissions. One could get sick over and over again.

Stage 5: They realize there is a finite number of drugs that could be utilized. They know that when drugs are not effective death is the result.

The children observed in the above stages needed the disease experience in order to pass from one stage to another stage. The understanding of the disease and its progression were not limited by age or intellectual ability. The children relied on their own experience of the illness and then on the sharing of information with peers involved in the same stage. "Some three and four year olds of average intelligence knew more about their prognosis than some very intelligent nine year olds who were still in their first remission. They were only aware of the fact that they had a serious illness." (Bluebond-Langner 1978, p. 169) The children's self concept also passed through five different stages that matched their understanding of the illness itself.

Stage 1: "I am seriously ill"

Stage 2: "I am seriously ill but I will get better"

Stage 3: "I am always ill but I will get better"

Stage 4: "I am always ill and I will not get better"

Stage 5: "I am dying"

Ken Doka in *Living with Life-Threatening Illness* defines that "a life threatening illness is any illness that endangers life or that has a significant risk of death. (Doka, 1993. p.xiv) Doka states that the experience of life-threatening illness can be viewed as a series of phases:

Pre-diagnosis Phase: This is the period prior to diagnosis when one suspects illness or risk. A child may complain of headaches, have bloody noses, fatigue or various physical symptoms.

Diagnostic Phase: This is an acutely stressful time when the illness is named. During this time, parents must cope with the crisis of possible death. Parents often say they feel there were two deaths. The first death would be at the time of terminal diagnosis, the second at the actual physical death.

Chronic Phase: In this phase, life goes on, including the medical and hospital visits, therapies, medication, physical changes and adaptation to the loss of familiar events and relationships.During this time, much energy is expended to keep things as normal as possible without denying the severity of the disease. Often the entire life of a family will need to integrate and adapt to the reality of a sick child while attempting to maintain some level of homeostasis and normalcy. This can be an extremely stressful period that requires careful attention to the needs of all the family members. Open communication and the need to grieve the losses that have already been experienced through the illness need to be acknowledged as well as incorporated into the reality that each day is precious and to be treasured for the memories being made.

Terminal Phase: The disease has moved to the point where death is inevitable. During this phase the emphasis is in providing pain-free treatment. Thus aggressive measures are not taken to prolong life, yet procedures and medications to relieve or reduce pain are prescribed.

Within each phase, physical, psychological and spiritual issues are raised by each individual. In respect of the individual process of addressing life-threatening illness, leading researchers in the field support the use of task-based models to assist in qualifying the patient's experience in each phase. (Corr, 1992; Corr & Doka, 1994; Doka 1993; Worden, 1991) Table 1 as found in Doka's *Living With*

Tasks in Life-Threatening Illness

General	Acute Phase	Chronic Phase	Terminal Phase
1. Responding to the physical fact of disease.	1. Understanding the disease	1. Managing symptoms and side effects	1. Dealing with symptoms, discomfort, pain, and incapacitation
2. Taking steps to cope with the reality of disease	2. Maximizing health and lifestyle 3. Maximizing one's coping strengths and limiting weaknesses 4. Developing strategies to deal with the issues created by the disease	2. Carrying out health regime 3. Preventing and managing health crisis 4. Managing stress and examining coping 5. Maximizing social support and minimizing isolation 6. Normalizing life in the face of the disease 7. Dealing with financial concerns	2. Managing health procedures and institutional stress 3. Managing stress and examining coping 4. Dealing effectively with caregivers 5. Preparing for death and saying goodbye
3. Preserving self concept and relationships with others in the face of disease	5. Exploring the effect of the diagnosis on a sense of self and others	8. Preserving self concept 9. Redefining relationships with others throughout the course of the disease	6. Preserving self concept 7. Preserving appropriate relationships with family and friends
4. Dealing with affective and existential/spiritual issues created or reactivated by the disease	6. Ventilating feelings and fears 7. Incorporating the present reality of diagnosis into one's sense of past and future	10. Ventilating feelings and fears 11. Finding meaning in suffering, chronicity, uncertainty, and decline	8. Ventilating feelings and fears 9. Finding meaning in life and death

Life-Threatening Illness outlines these tasks within each phase of the process. In general the four tasks are as follows:

Task 1: Respond to the physical fact of disease.
Task 2: Take steps to cope with the reality of the disease.
Task 3: Preserve self-concept and relationships with others in the face of disease.
Task 4: Dealing with effective and existential spiritual issues created or reactivated by the disease.

Within each phase these tasks take on specific qualities pertaining to the individual needs of the child. Thus within the terminal phase the tasks would be as follows:

1. Dealing with symptoms, discomfort, pain and incapacitation.
2. Managing health procedures and institutional stress.
3. Managing stress and examining coping.
4. Dealing effectively with caregivers.
5. Preparing for death and saying goodbye.
6. Preserving self concept.
7. Preserving appropriate relationships with family and friends.
8. Ventilating feelings and fears.
9. Finding meaning in life and death.

The tasks in the diagnostic phase take on a different face than those in the terminal phase. A thirteen year old girl in end stage AIDS residing on a hospice unit or in home will need to rely more on the help of caregivers in the terminal phase than in the diagnostics or chronic phase. Dealing with the embarrassment of wearing a diaper, or not being able to apply her own lipstick (for example) are tasks dealing with self concept that earlier were not problematic. Later in the chapter we will see how these tasks may also be influenced by the developmental milestones of each age.

Children, as adults, will cope with the above tasks when facing life-threatening illness. Yet there are some qualifiers and special concerns within the worlds of children.

The first qualifier is that children are often protected by being told they are ill or denied the opportunity to speak of their understanding of the illness or thoughts of dying. Parents or caregivers in some circumstances may share the name of the illness, yet reserve facts or limit discussion of the prognosis. The primary question from my hospice experience becomes who is being served in the situation? If a child is cognitively aware and asks questions regarding the illness or death and dying, it seems an injustice to deny or edit discussion. On a level comfortable to the child and following the lead of the child's interest, thoughts, fantasies, feelings and concerns need to be explored. Having worked on a hospice unit it is of interest to note that children will often discuss the issues of their illness or potential death with caregivers, even when the parents have reserved sharing the full prognosis of the illness. It appears that the child is trying to protect the parent or guardian just as much as the parents are protecting the child. Often children will share information with staff or alternate caregivers if they feel there is a receptive and trusting attitude and if they are consistently present to them. Often this sharing of feelings or thoughts regarding their illness comes without warning. It may seemingly come out of nowhere and not even be in anticipation of a response. One boy while being fed one evening looked up and said to the technician, "I won't be here for my birthday." The technician replied, "Where are you going?" In response the boy said, "I'm going to see my grandpa." His grandpa had died several months prior and it was evident they had been very close. However the boy did not choose to discuss the issue any further and continued to eat without any evidence of discomfort or emotional distress. This example further indicates that children do have an inner awareness of their illness and impending death. (Bluebond-Langner 1978, Kubler-Ross, 1983)

Children may show an inner awareness of their illness or terminal condition not only through direct verbal communication but also through play, art, and musical expressions. Elisabeth Kubler-Ross addresses this inner knowing in her book *On Children and Death.* "If people doubt that their children are aware of a terminal illness, they should look at the poems or drawings these children create, often during their illness but sometimes months before a diagnosis is made. It needs to be understood that there is often a pre-conscious awareness and not a conscious, intellectual knowledge. It comes from the `inner spiritual, intuitive quadrant' and gradually prepares the child to face the forthcoming transition even if the grownups deny or avoid the reality."(Kubler-Ross, 1983. p.134) The following is a personal experience with a terminally ill child that demonstrates the power of art communication and the benefits of therapeutically utilizing music and visualization for pain reduction.

Mary drew the picture (on the next page) a week prior to her death following a visit where I utilized music and guided visualization (hypnotherapy) techniques. She was having much difficulty breathing and was in obvious physical distress even with the oxygen mask in place. Gently strumming my guitar I began to create a story inviting Mary to journey to a land where there were beautiful flowers, and children playing in sunshine, freely breathing in the spring air. Visibly responding to the imagery and hypnotherapy in conjunction with the music, within fifteen minutes Mary was breathing much more comfortably. In addition to the positive response Mary exhibited I also had the gift of a song from spending this healing time with her. The words came as follows and is entitled *Bring Rainbows to the Children.*

Bring flowers to the children
Bring flowers to the children
Bring flowers to the children
Bring flowers and love.

Bring many splendid colors
Bring many splendid colors
Bring many splendid colors
Bring colors and love

And dance upon the mountains
And skip upon the green green grass
Feel the earth beneath your feet
and look up to the sky
And drink in all the sunshine
And feel the breeze that moves the trees
Pick a cloud that has your name
and float on way up high

Bring rainbows to the children
Bring rainbows to the children
Bring rainbows to the children
Bring rainbows and love

Bring many splendid colors
Bring many splendid colors

Bring many splendid colors
Bring colors and love

With Mary seemingly more comfortable I asked if she would like to
draw a picture: She immediately responded and within several minutes
handed me her creation. She indicated
that she wanted me to keep it. She
could not verbally speak at this time,
so I could not discuss it further with
her. Several months following her
death I shared the picture with a col-
league familiar with art interpretation. He said that the owl is known
to be a symbol of death. In her own way Mary let me know that she
knew what was happening. This experience among many others
has taught me to trust the use of alternate creative modalities in
gaining access to the intuitive and unconscious wellsprings that
speak loudly if we listen.

Developmental Levels of the Child

When deciding how to communicate information to a child regarding the illness, Doka has earlier addressed three primary questions: What does a child need to know? What does a child want to
know, and what can a child understand? In pondering these questions it is also helpful to be aware of the developmental level of the
child. The developmental level will impact on how the child responds and copes with the illness. As William Easson states in *The
Dying Child:* "The best treatment of the dying youngster can be based
only on the knowledge of what his approaching death means to
him and how this young patient can reasonably cope with this very
personal reality. (Easson, 1970. p.5)

Newborn and infants are not able to conceptualize illness. They
are concerned with immediate events dealing with pain and trauma.
They also fear separation from the mother. The developmental task
of achieving differentiation from mother and a sense of self awareness may be affected because of the sometimes necessary periods of
separation due to hospitalization. Even in cases where a child is
developmentally delayed or has serious birth defects, the power of

a mothers touch is remarkable and necessary. As much as possible the mother and father should remain connected through touching the child, as well as talking to and being present to the child.

The toddler's task is of gaining self control and autonomy. The physical limits on a child due to an illness may affect the developing sense of self. It is best to maintain normal schedule times and consistent limitations while understanding the stressors and realities of the illness. A toddler will not have an understanding of death, yet will understand pain and feel anxiety and separation. Allowing a child to engage in regular play activities honors autonomy and self control while also providing therapeutic release.

The pre-schooler is finding a way in the world with a developing sense of exploration. Thus sickness and hospitalization may be seen as a form of punishment. Caregivers need to reassure the child that they have done nothing wrong or bad to warrant acquiring this illness. The preschooler will take words quite literally. Be truthful about medical procedures and in language that will not be misinterpreted. Deal on the basis of the here and now, communicating simply and honestly. When a child is in the end stage of life, parents should tolerate and support regression to a more infantile stage and assure him always of their love.

The school age child is learning to be independent and self confident assuming new responsibilities and wider boundaries. The school age child is often aware of illness and terminal condition without being told. They are aware of the concept of death and understand the nuances of their illness. A child in this age group can face the prospect of death with the support, comfort and understanding of his family and friends. Open and honest communication should be ongoing with opportunities for the child to talk about fears and concerns, needs and wishes.

The adolescent with an emerging self identity is more independent and autonomous. Peer relationships and sexual identity and understanding are primary issues during these years.

Their privacy needs to be respected even when it is necessary to depend on caregivers for personal care. They understand the finality of death and can be concerned about the needs and reactions of family members. Adolescents coping with life-threatening illness can face additional stresses when it affects their physical looks. They benefit from the support of peers and should be involved in decision making regarding their care. (Easson, 1970, Weiner, Fair, Pizzo, 1993)

Communicating with Children facing life-threatening illness

Spinetta (1977, 1978, 1980) believes it is best to address the issue of the seriousness of the illness from the time of diagnosis. Although increased medical advances have helped to increase the life-span of terminally ill children it is best to answer children's questions with reality based hope and optimism. The task of telling a child about a life-threatening diagnosis, medical treatments, and a potentially shortened life span is a challenging and painful thought. Within the mindset of open and honest communication the how-to's of telling a child are not at all black and white. Spinetta's five viewpoints or prerequisites can be helpful to review prior to speaking with a child regarding issues of life-threatening illness:

1) The parent's philosophical stance on death, and
2) the parent's emotional stance on death.

One needs to understand the family's view of life and death and integrate that in discussions with the child. Has there been a death in the family or other serious illness? How did people react and communicate around those issues. What was the child's involvement? How did people express their grief? I always ask families what the child knows (as well as the siblings) and what their hopes are at the time. Often parents understand the terminal status yet are hesitant or unwilling to discuss it with the child. I offer assistance in this matter as is comfortable with the family. If the family is strongly opposed to discussing death with the child, I ask permission for other careproviders to respond as the issue arises.

3) A child's age, experience and level of development.

A child's concept and understanding of death are affected by age, experience, intellectual ability and development.

4) Family coping strategies

How a family deals with crises will be an indicator of how they will cope with a life-threatening illness in the family. An understanding of psychological, behavioral, social, and spiritual resource's utilized in the past can assist the family in creating a coping system.

5) Child's Affinity For Process Over Content

Children are aware of how a message is communicated as well as the behavior exhibited. What one says is not as important as the non-verbal and emotional cues which a child picks up on. "Unless someone explains to children, at their level, what is happening, the children may have imagined fears, distresses, and concerns that are much more disturbing and difficult to deal with than the actual facts." (Spinetta, 1981. p. 239)

Spinetta's work clearly indicates that open communication regarding the illness better sustained and supported the child prior to death, as well as the family during the mourning process.

Hospice as a Concept of Care for Children

Dr. Neil Lombardi, Medical Director of St. Mary's Hospital for Children, which has a ten bed hospice unit reserved for terminally ill children, states the following regarding the subject of death in childhood: "When I first entered pediatric residency training, the subject of death in childhood was not a topic of discussion. It was generally considered that the objective of all our ministrations was the survival of the child, no matter how ill, at all costs." (Lombardi, 1993. p.248) Yet, despite the most advanced medical treatments children do die. In many cases there comes a point where aggressive medical intervention to cure is no longer useful or appropriate.

The success of St. Mary's Hospital for Children's Palliative Care Unit supports the proof of the benefits of a hospice philosophy for terminally ill children. This philosophy can exist within the confines of an In-patient unit, or in a home-care setting. In either case, the child and the family are the unit of care. Parents suffer profoundly and benefit not only from the physical care provided for the child, but also the psychological, emotional, spiritual care available through the team approach. As Ann Armstrong-Dailey, founder of Children's Hospice International states: "Children's hospice care provides much-needed services by encouraging the ongoing involvement of family members and health care professionals with the dying child, and implementing practical knowledge of effective and appropriate palliative measures in children with life-threatening conditions." (Armstrong-Dailey, 1991, p. 226)

Choosing hospice or palliative care for a child does not mean abandoning hope. Although a six month to one year life expectancy is a guide for the admission process, our team has helped many children and families who have outlived that "limit". Children with certain congenital malformations, anencephaly or hydranencephaly who were expected to live for days lived for years. In other cases, children with the same diagnosis died within the period of expectancy. Yet, accepting a hospice way of care does not mean letting go of hope, love support, or involvement. At a time of life when guarantees are no longer granted it embraces the child and the family in a network and cocoon of optimal care.

A young father responded to the doctor's honest prognosis that rehabilitative therapies could not bring the child to walk again by exclaiming: "How do you know that? Anything is possible!" And although this father knelt and prayed with a hope and belief in a miracle, this child and family still benefitted from the hospice care provided. They benefitted from the physician who prescribed the pain and symptom control medications and daily observed the child. They benefitted from the nursing care that allowed them the time and flexibility to adjust their work schedules to have someone with their son as much as possible. They benefitted from the therapeutic services offered by the social worker who assisted with financial concerns and also with their feelings of anguish, guilt and fear. They benefitted from the pastoral care chaplain who supported them on their spiritual journey and in their questioning "Why me?" They benefitted from the music therapist who provided music of relaxation, stimulation, pain management and therapeutic release. They benefitted from the speech, occupational and physical therapists available for consultation and services to provide comfort and quality of life exercises. They benefitted from the on site school and educational stimulation and interaction with peers. They benefitted from the volunteers who were supportive companions ready to cuddle, read a book, or hold a hand.

In addition to all the specialized services and benefits of care provided, there is an understanding and knowledge that all the families being served are grieving and doing their best to survive the nightmare! Yet, hope is never abandoned. As the illness progresses it may change its face. Hope for a miracle may become hope that the child gets to enjoy one more Christmas. Finally, there is hope that the family will be present at the actual time of death and that it be peaceful.

The benefits of hospice care for children require flexibility and ongoing individual assessment.

> It is not necessary or even practical to consider the decision to seek palliative care as mutually exclusive of ongoing treatment, and indeed the values involved suggest a more reasonable 'dovetailing' of the concepts to allow flexibility. There is no reason, for example, to exclude a child with AIDS and wasting syndrome from palliative care services because the child is receiving total parenteral nutrition even though the treatment might prolong the survival time of the child. Thoughtful considerations of this nature will serve to prevent the exclusion of many children from hospice services until the last minute when neither they nor their families can benefit from such services or they can no longer psychologically take advantage of palliative care. (Lombardi, 1993. p. 251)

Children and families in the terminal illness can benefit from hospice care. No child should die isolated in a corner room of a hospital because of the difficult feelings that arise when confronting death and our fragility. Hospice recognizes dying as a process which affirms life. Those working with children and their families need to be specifically trained and sensitive to the complexities of the psychosocial, medical and spiritual needs within the system being served.

Hospice has always been sensitive to the bereavement process. The death of a child for the parents, siblings and extended family raises unique issues requiring knowledge and compassion for those living through this complicated loss. Thus, the Hospice team faces the additional challenge of not only learning about life through the eyes of a dying child, but also understanding how the death of a child impacts on the surviving family members. This knowledge will greatly serve to help create moments of meaning and memory on a road that often is lonely and devastatingly painful.

Conclusion

There is no reason why children should have to face life-threatening illnesses. There is no reason why a child should die. As we raise our fists to the heavens we should not allow our anger to remove us from the children who need our understanding, constancy and honesty. There is no one perfect way to walk the road of life-threatening or terminal illness with a child. Yet there are ways. Keep walking and keep talking and listen patiently. Walk always with your eyes and ears open to the child. Look and listen and respect that on conscious and unconscious levels the child is very involved in the process. Be loving. Be supportive. Be there. The child will lead you.

References

Armstrong-Dailey, A. (1991). Hospice care for children: Their families and health care providers. In D. Papadatou & C. Papadatos (Eds.) *Children and death.* New York: Hemisphere Publishing Co.

Backer, B., & Nannon, N., & Russell, N. (1994). Death and dying:understanding and care. Delmar Publishers.

Blechar Gibbons, Martha. (1993). Psychosocial aspects of serious illness in childhood and adolescence. In A. Armstrong-Dailey

& S. Zarbock Goltzer (Eds.) *Hospice care for children* (pp.61-73). New York: Oxford University Press.

Bluebond-Langner, M. (1989). Worlds of dying children and their well siblings. *Death Studies,* 13;1-16, 1989.

Buckingham, R. (1983). *The complete hospice guide.* New York: Harper & Row.

Corr, C.A. (1992). A task-based approach to coping with dying. *Omega,* 24, 81-94.

Doka, K.J. (1993) Living with life-threatening illness: A guide for patients, their families, and caregivers. Lexington, MA: Lexington Books.

Easson, W. (1970). *The dying child.* Illinois: Charles C. Thomas.

Gyulay, J. (1989). Home care for the dying child. *Issues in Comprehensive Pediatric Nursing,* 12:33-69.

Kovach, N. (1994). Pediatric palliative in-patient care at St. Mary's hospital for children: Marketing Mix analysis and implications of health care reform. Final paper for class MH334-New School for Social Research.

Kübler-Ross, E. (1983). *On children and death.* New York: Macmillan Publishing Co.

Lombardi, N. (1993) Palliative care in an in-patient setting. In A. Armstrong-Dailey & S. Zarbock Goltzer (Eds.),

Hospice care for children (pp248-265). New York: Oxford University Press.

Martinson, I. (1993). Hospice care for children: Past, present & future. *Journal of pediatric oncology nursing,* 10, No.3, 93-98.

Papadatou, D. & Papadatos, C. (Eds). (1991) *Children and death.* New York: Hemisphere Publishing Co.

Spinetta, J. (1974). The dying child's awareness of death: A review: *Psychological bulletin,* Vol 81, No. 4, 256-260.

Spinetta, J.J., & Deasy-Spinetta, P. (Eds.). (1981). Living with childhood cancer. St. Louis: C.V. Mosby.

Wilson, Dottie. (1988). The ultimate loss: The dying child. In Dying and disabled children: Dealing with loss & grief. New York: The Haworth Press.

Wiener, L., & Fari, C. & Pizzo, P. (1993) Care for the child with HIV infection and AIDS. In A Armstrong Dailey & S. Zarbock Goltzer (Eds.), *Hospice care for children* (PP.85-104). New York: Oxford University Press.

Children and HIV: Orphans and Victims

5

Gary R. Anderson

Introduction

In the early 1980s, soon after the first adults with Acquired Immunodeficiency Syndrome (AIDS) were identified, a number of children began to evidence similar symptoms. The U.S. Centers for Disease Control and Prevention affirmed that children were getting AIDS. By June 1994, over 5,700 children under the age of thirteen in the United States were diagnosed with AIDS.

The virus believed to cause AIDS, Human Immunodeficiency Virus (HIV), is transmitted from mother to infant during pregnancy, in childbirth, or, in rare cases, through breast milk. In a small number of cases children have become HIV-infected due to contact with infected blood or semen when sexually-abused by an adult man. For adolescents, the means of transmission could be similar to adult transmission through contact with infected blood, semen, or vaginal fluids. Contact due to blood is most frequently due to intravenous drug-use and needle sharing.

Children with HIV have a number of nonspecific symptoms, including: enlarged lymph nodes, enlarged liver and spleen, oral thrush, diarrhea, weight loss, and fever. There are also other signs that may indicate HIV infection and progression to AIDS: a seriously compromised immune system, opportunistic infections such as types of pneumonia, serious bacterial infections, neurological changes, and organ damage. Medical treatment includes preventive interventions, for example, using antibiotics to lessen the likelihood of acquiring pneumonia or medications to slow the progression of the virus. There are also therapies to support the immune system. Early and aggressive treatment of infections and illnesses is very important, as well as addressing the child's nutrition.

In addition to children with HIV/AIDS, there has been a growing awareness of the impact of AIDS on children who are not infected but have a family member or friend who has HIV/AIDS. It is estimated that over 100,000 children will be AIDS orphans by the year 2,000. This chapter will briefly identify some of the multiple issues for children with HIV/AIDS and affected by AIDS.

Children with HIV/AIDS

There are a number of issues that face the child and family with HIV/AIDS: (1) testing and treatment; (2) developmental needs; (3) disclosure; and (4) the need for a caregiver.

Testing and Treatment.

Should a child be tested for HIV and if so, when? An infant born to a mother with HIV infection may or may not be infected with the virus. The infant receives the mother's antibodies in the uterus before birth or during birth. Consequently, a newborn would test positive for HIV antibodies and up to his/her second year. The number of children who are actually HIV-infected at birth is estimated to be 25 percent. As infants become older, the majority will seroconvert—testing negative for HIV. Some will test positive—and may develop symptoms—indicating that the infection is their own. With preventive therapies, early identification of HIV status may have significant benefits. The mandatory HIV testing of pregnant women is a controversial issue weighing the privacy and rights of mothers, and the best interests of children, among other considerations. There may also be issues related to medical care, including when to use AZT, or the use of experimental medications and strategies. An important issue in the medical response and management of the illness is whether or not the child and family have access to a knowledgeable medical team, and the availability of other services for the family.

Developmental Needs.

One of the key issues for children who have HIV/AIDS is to prevent or minimize the impact of the disease and its medical treatment from overly interfering with the child's development. To the extent possible, the child who has HIV should be kept in the mainstream of a family's life, so that the child can receive the stimulation and nurturing that are the basic needs of all infants and young children. The child's normal developmental needs continue despite the

HIV infection. Children are living for many years after HIV infection, even when the infection takes place before or at birth.

For example, there were three early adolescent girls who had been HIV-infected since birth. They were regularly followed at a hospital clinic where the nurses and social workers developed a close relationship with the girls and their families over the years. The girls wanted to find a way to be involved with other people—to be helpful and make a contribution with their lives. They applied to become hospital volunteers, requesting to work in the pediatric playroom. The girls' request was approved. After they began their work, they reported to the social worker that these were among the happiest days of their lives.

There are a number of obstacles to addressing the child's normal developmental needs. First, the child may have frequent and persistent illnesses. Even such common childhood diseases as chicken pox or the measles can pose life-threatening complications or prove stubbornly difficult to overcome. Ear and throat infections, diarrhea, and other conditions may make it difficult for a child to be actively involved with one's family or community. AIDS is a chronic disease that can weaken the child physically and emotionally.

Second, even when the child is not ill, there may be frequent and regular medical check-ups and preventive medical treatments requiring hospital and clinic visits. This can be very time and energy-consuming and create a social world and life for the child at a medical facility. Due to time and intensity of contact, the nurses, physicians, social workers, and other personnel may have a significant social role in the child's life.

Third, one of the possible results of HIV can be neurological damage due to an infection of the brain. Studies of children have found widely varying estimates of the number of children whose central nervous systems have been affected by HIV, ranging from less than 10 percent to over 50 percent of children studied. The result of infection of the brain in children can result in loss of language, gross and fine motor skills, and thinking ability. Some children also have brain tumors or are at risk for strokes. In addition to HIV, cognitive ability may also be negatively affected by complications due to the exposure to drugs, such as cocaine, or to malnutrition.

Another potential obstacle to attending to the child's developmental needs may be the impairment of the parent. The mode of transmissions for the majority of children with AIDS has been from an infected mother. The parent's ability to care for the child may be compromised by their own HIV-related illness, other health problems, or circumstances related to drug-use or other economic or social stresses.

Despite these obstacles, children with HIV and AIDS need to have their developmental needs addressed. Some of the obstacles, such as neurological complications, are associated with a formal diagnosis of AIDS. The HIV-infected child may have no symptoms or signs of illness. The issue remains—how to maximize one's life within the need for vigilant preventive medicine for a chronic condition, and at times, intensive intervention for a life-threatening illness.

Disclosure.

A prominent issue for children and families with HIV/AIDS is whom to tell, if anyone, about the child's condition. There have been cautions about telling other people about one's HIV status. This is a diagnosis that is often accompanied by stigma and discrimination. There have been episodes of children being barred from school, isolated at school, and families being harassed and driven from communities by fearful neighbors. There are confidentiality laws to protect the child and family from disclosure and require that professionals not disclose the child or family's medical condition without the family's explicit and informed consent.

The child and family's own sense of stigma, guilt, or failure may reinforce a desire to keep one's HIV status an individual or family secret. The risk of discrimination makes this secretiveness understandable and perhaps necessary but it can result in a social isolation that complicates the emotional issues facing a child and family. The anger and sorrow of illness and suffering are compounded by a secrecy that doesn't allow the potential support and encouragement that some in the child's environment might offer. The relief of expressing one's thoughts and feelings that often accompanies grieving and crisis is silenced due to fear, and resulting isolation. At times, this isolation may become more troublesome than facing potential discrimination.

An assessment of who needs to know the child's medical condition is an important issue to be discussed with one's medical team or other confidants. Some people may need to know the child's status in order to be appropriately helpful. The child and family may want to tell selected others so they can receive the support that is helpful in times of stress and crisis. As the disclosure of the child's HIV status is an almost automatic disclosure of the mother's status as well, the disclosure decision and the scope of the people informed will have an impact on the entire family system, not just the child.

Caregivers.

A child with HIV/AIDS may need a consistent caregiver and home. Because the child's mother is also infected and may be very ill, the parent may be unable to care for the child. This inability to care for the child may be episodic, for example, during a hospital-ization of the parent due to acute illness, or long-term if the parent is very ill or rundown. If the parent cannot care for the child a rela-tive, or friend, may be identified who can take care of the child. This may not be easy as such persons may not be willing to care for the child, or the family's illness and life style may have isolated them from possible sources of support in their family or community.

The child may need a new home. If the parent cannot take care of the child, and there are no available relatives or friends, the child may be placed in a foster home. In a number of communities in the United States there are specialized foster care programs with foster parents who have been specially trained and sensitized to care for children with HIV/ AIDS.

Other Issues.

For older children with HIV/AIDS there are issues related to the prevention of the transmission of HIV and protection of the per-son from further exposure to the virus or other illnesses. This in-cludes prevention education and the importance of such choices as abstinence from risky behaviors, and behaviors that are safe or safer.

Children Affected by AIDS

There are a number of issues that confront children who do not have HIV but are in families where either one or more family mem-bers have HIV or AIDS. Affected children are sometimes called AIDS orphans, as they outlive their infected parents. Although the child does not have HIV/AIDS, he or she will be profoundly affected because their mother, perhaps also their father and brothers or sisters are infected. The affected child also includes those children with extended family members and "chosen" family members with HIV/ AIDS. The issues facing affected children are similar to those facing infected children—infected children are also affected children with at least a mother with HIV/AIDS.

The significant difference is that the affected child is usually not coping with their own life-threatening and chronic illness at the same time. But this should not in any way minimize the physical, psychological, and social challenges that confront the affected child. For example, even though the affected child does not have HIV, the child still may have health and physical complications due to the parent's drug use during pregnancy, or malnutrition or neglect after birth. More likely than with the infected child, this child will be expected to carry at least some if not an inordinate burden of responsibility for the family. This might include performing physical tasks as well as providing attention and emotional support and supervision for other children and the parent. This role reversal with the parent sets up expectations for the child that may be difficult to achieve, or can be achieved at the cost of one's own development and childhood activities.

As with the infected child, the affected child will often be instructed to maintain secrecy concerning the parent's and sibling's illness. The child may not even be informed of the parent's illness until the parent is gravely ill, if at all. The child with the high probability of being orphaned is facing a challenge that is emotionally formidable for any child. This challenge is made all the more dangerous by the nature of the illness—AIDS—and frequently the context of the ill family—poverty, discrimination, and a stressed community.

For the child with a family member(s) with AIDS, the sense of loss and grief may begin considerably before the person becomes gravely ill or dies. There will be episodic times of acute illness in which the person will be very ill and possibly near death but able to recover after an emergency hospitalization. The affected child repeatedly is confronted with the parent or sibling's death only to gain a respite until another crisis. There is also the loss of a functioning family member, as the ill person may be depressed, withdrawn, or bedridden due to a variety of wasting illnesses. The person is in many ways lost to the child although still alive. The person with AIDS may also have a specific neurological disease that would affect cognitive ability, resulting in the loss of the parent due to a confused and disoriented state. Without assistance, it may be difficult for the child to have pleasant memories of a family member who has had a chronic and debilitating illness.

One of the critical issues and processes for children is related to grieving, and its complications due to HIV/AIDS:

◆ In bereavement, *children need to understand what is happening and what has happened to them and their loved ones.* With AIDS, there may have been no communication within the family due to stigma, shame, guilt, or being overwhelmed with many life circumstances. The family may not be organized or accustomed to talking about problems, particularly of this magnitude. Even when there are conversations within the family, the participants might be limited to adults, believing that children either would not understand or need to be sheltered from the information. This secretiveness could increase a child's apprehensions as they are aware that something is happening but the causes and consequences are not clarified. In this atmosphere, a child is free to create and imagine a range of frightening possibilities, including blaming themselves for their family's misery.

◆ In bereavement, *children need to express an emotional response in anticipation to a loss and/or during and after a loss.* Again the family's secrecy or exclusion of the child would shortcut any anticipatory grieving. Even when the child is aware of the losses in the family, the child's emotional response might be muted to preserve the family's secret in the community, or repressed as the child continues or assumes significant responsibilities in the family. The general level of stress in the family might make it difficult for any adult to attend to the feelings of a grief-stricken and confused child. The adults' own grief and guilt might dominate their response to the loss and make it difficult to be attuned to the child's world and needs.

◆ A grieving process is helped by a *commemoration of the loss of the loved person in some formal and informal manner.* These rituals that encourage remembering and community support are often expressed in the context of religion. However, in many families, their previous life style and stressors, such as drug use, may have alienated the family from a religious community. There may also be negative attitudes toward AIDS, associating the illness with homosexuality and drug use, and other practices not accepted by a religious community. With a loss of a formal community, there may not be a replacement so the child and family have a void of rituals to commemorate and mark the death of a family member.

◆ The grieving process includes *learning how to go on with one's life.* This learning and reconstruction for children requires the support of caring adults, the presence of role models, and assistance in constructing some sense of meaning to what one has experienced and one's ongoing identity and sense of purpose in life. This is a significant challenge for anyone, particularly a child experiencing multiple stressors, with minimal social support, and considerable emotional distress that is pent up inside. It would not be unlikely that a lonely child would worry about his/her own existence, find the world to be a very unsafe and hostile place to live, define parents and adults in general as at least unreliable.

◆ The death of a parent can also have profound *psychological repercussions as there may be guilt and remorse in addition to the sorrow and anger*. The child's ambivalence about the parent, particularly the ill and seemingly inattentive parent, may complicate their response to the parent's loss. With the death of a sibling, there may also be complications due to sibling rivalry and survivor guilt—why did one have AIDS and the other one was spared? Did one's angry wishes and fantasies contribute to the death of a parent or sibling? Experiencing a traumatic life event may lead to recurring feelings of anxiety, even the sense of reexperiencing the loss, resulting in trouble sleeping, and a continual sense of alertness and sense of being threatened and insecure.

◆ The illness of a family member and death are often accompanied *by spiritual issues and concerns* for children. Why did this person die, why did they become ill to begin with, where are they now, and what will happen to me? These questions are challenging to caregivers and faith communities who might struggle to respond and support a child. There may not be such supports available to the child; there may not be persons who are sensitive and attentive to the spiritual dimension of the child's response to loss.

The death of a parent can have multiple dramatic effects on all areas of a child's life. The loss of a parent might require moving to the home of a relative or friend. It may also mean being placed in foster care with a new and unknown family. These moves can dislocate the child—removing them from a neighborhood, school, friends, landmarks, and connections that provided at least familiarity if not security and comfort. For older children it may mean living on their own, or assuming responsibility for younger siblings. Even younger children will be pressed into responsible adult-like roles with younger children.

Conclusion

For many children and families, these and other issues are compounded by a context of violence, homelessness, drug and alcohol use, poverty, community stresses and discrimination. AIDS may be one more problem that is added to a number of other challenges. The impact of AIDS is profound enough to pressure families with multiple resources and few additional difficulties. Children have multiple reasons for grief, and face a complicated mourning process. Social support is crucial so that children can have a measure of resiliency and the capacity to mourn and live.

References:

Gary R. Anderson. *Courage to Care: Responding to the Crisis of Children with AIDS*. Washington, DC: CWLA, 1990.

Barbara Dane and Carol Levine. *AIDS and the New Orphans: Coping with Death*. Westport, CN: Auburn House, 1994.

Child Welfare League of America. *Meeting the Challenge of HIV Infection in Family Foster Care*. Washington, DC: CWLA, 1991.

P. Brouwers, A. Belman, and L. Epstein. (1991) "Central Nervous System Involvement" In P. Pizzo and C. Wilfret (eds.) *Pediatric AIDS*, Baltimore: Williams and Wilkens, pp. 318-335.

Section Three
Children Mourning, Mourning Children

Children mourning, as well as parents and others mourning children, have an inevitable sense of pathos. In a perfect world, we would wish children unsullied by death. But in our world, children do die and even more experience loss in a variety of forms.

Catherine Sanders, a noted grief therapist, begins with an overview of the grieving process as experienced by children and adults. Sanders reminds us that children may experience grief in different ways than adults. She also notes the critical role that adults can play in the child's life at this time, a point reinforced by all the articles in the section. Sanders also sensitively explores the nature of parental loss. It is not helpful to grade losses, to suggest that certain losses are worse than others. Each loss creates its own special pain. In that sense, Sanders explores the unique difficulties posed by the loss of a child. Sanders also offers a schema of the grieving process, reminding us that it too can be a roller coaster of emotions, periods when one thinks one is doing better as well as times when one experiences sustained sadness.

Ronald Barrett's brief chapter builds on Sander's themes. Barrett reviews the ways that circumstances such as traumatic loss can complicate the experience of grief. Barrett's chapter also emphasizes the ways that class and culture can affect a child's experiences with death. Persons interested in further exploring trauma may wish to consult Raphael's (*When Disaster Strikes*) classic work as well as the abundant literature on trauma and critical incident stress debriefing, a technique often used with persons experiencing trauma.

Stephen Hersh's chapter offers a bridge between the chapters in this section. He, too, reviews the particular ways that children may express grief. But Hersh's chapter also emphasizes sources of help for the grieving child. He affirms Sanders and Barrett's points about the need for supportive adults. This is often a challenge since adults too may be grieving. But Hersh also reminds that peers can provide critical assistance during this time.

These themes are carried forth by Robert Stevenson who stresses the supportive roles schools can have in helping a grieving child. And together Hersh and Stevenson add a comforting idea. Neither parents nor their children have to, or should, face loss alone.

References

Raphael, Beverly. (1986). *When Disaster Strikes.* NY: Basic Books.

Grief of Children and Parents   6

Catherine M. Sanders

The Child's Experience of Grief

Do children grieve? A bettor question would be "Do we allow children to grieve." There is no doubt as to the first question. Evidence has shown that babies even as young as six months manifest early signs of separation anxiety when they find themselves without their primary caregiver for any length or time.

As to the second question, there is also compelling evidence to indicate that adults do very often exclude children from their own grief experiences. They do this in many ways, usually in the name of the child's protection, but often it is actually for the adult's own protection. Several reasons have been cited:

- When a death occurs communication within the family breaks down
- Parents and other adults are distraught and emotionally absent from other children
- There is high anxiety and general upheaval in the home
- Strangers and visitors fill the home
- Absence of the dead parent or sibling

These reasons, coupled with the possibility that children may be sent away to another house for a few days, is firm basis for inordinate trauma to the children.

At the same time, children may be told a variety of things about the dead parent or sibling as to where they have gone. Statements such as "She has gone to heaven to be with God," or "He is visiting a friend in another city" are often given. Any number of things come to mind all leading the child to a state of confusion and away from the thing he needs the most; an honest answer about what has happened, a loving protective arm around him, and some encouragement to share his own feelings.

The parents themselves may be too shocked and grief stricken to even recognize that their child needs them. So often the interaction with remaining children is left to others. In one case, a six year-old sibling, whose bother was suddenly killed, hid herself in a closet and was not missed for an entire day. She had simply been forgotten in the general upheaval of the household and in her own terror had tried to seek comfort in a dark safe place.

Since the family represents security and safety to the child, when this safety is disrupted, the child will feel insecure, highly anxious, robbed of the consistent world to which she had been accustomed.

Parents often fail to recognize signs of grief or sadness, particularly in the small child. The young child may go back to bed wetting or cry for the bottle again. Regressive clinging behavior or self isolation may be a key to the fact that the child needs comforting. So often these types of behavior are seen only that the child is acting babyish and, as a result, is often reprimanded for these actions.

Developmental issues play a large part in identifying bereavement behavior in children. Recognizing that cognitive and emotional areas, not to mention physical and social functioning, are in a constant state of flux, it is hard to describe childhood bereavement patterns in one single descriptive statement. Grief is not a static process, particularly with children. Just as adult patterns of grieving are dependent on many external and internal moderators, the child is affected by these moderator variables as well. However, the younger child suffers an additional problem in that when adults attempt to protect him by not talking about the death, the child suffers from inadequate knowledge and imagines the worst possible situation. Magical thinking will be prominent. The child might be saying a nighttime prayer such as;

> Now I lay me down to sleep,
> I pray the Lord my soul to keep,
> If I should die before I wake,
> I pray the Lord my soul to take.

It may have been that this particular prayer had been said habitually until a death occurred. Now the young child is afraid to even close his eyes for fear the Lord might "keep" his soul. What happens at the time of death, how and what the child is told will be of utmost importance in helping him over this most difficult hurdle.

Latency

As the child matures into latency (6 to 12), there appears a developing capacity for guilt The child worries about what has happened or what might happen. Because of this, she might feel a sense of responsibility for the death. She may have secretly wished at an earlier time in a fit of anger for a sibling or even a parent to "drop dead." When the death happened, the developing conscience gives rise to guilty self torture. It is very difficult for a child to share these very natural, but to her, ugly thoughts and feelings.

At the same time, the period of latency brings with it a natural calm and the child learns to control his feelings with greater equanimity. Emotions move from external acting out to quieter internal control. The child around eight or nine may carry on as if nothing has happened, laughing and playing as usual. This behavior may be misread as not caring and as a result cost him the comforting he would otherwise receive.

For the school aged child, attending classes might be a problem because he wants to be like other kids and the recent death in the family can make him seem different. The child may try to hide the information from other students or on the other hand, he may put on a show of bravado to cover up the painful feelings he is experiencing. It has been seen that girls will often become excessive caregivers in an effort to hide their sadness.

As the child moves toward puberty, an emerging adult-like grieving behavior is seen. The future appears as a reality, stronger than before and she becomes aware of the frightening reality of her own possible demise. The older child, when the parent is absent, either through death or emotionally withdrawn, now is equipped to share some of her thoughts with teachers or other close adults, thereby gaining access to support and nurturing outside the family. This is particularly helpful when one or both parents have died. It has been shown in children, just as it has in adults, that the availability of person and social resources often make the difference in positive bereavement outcome.

Family Relationships

For all children at all ages, family relationships both before and after the death contribute heavily to the way a child views death.

When the child is socialized in a family where death is never discussed, the child's fears build and he resorts to magical thinking. Feelings are never dealt with and the child carries the taboo of death on into adult life. It is then passed on to future generations.

For families that are open and talk to one another about their feelings, the child has the greatest opportunity to assimilate the sadness of grief without becoming overwhelmed with fear. Growing up in such a family allows the child to openly discuss his anger or sadness and still know that he will be comforted. He is hurt but not frightened for he knows that loss and pain can be acknowledged.

However, an open family does not immunize one from pain. As a matter of fact, the intensity of grief is greater simply because the open family allows true feelings to manifest themselves without holding back. Somehow, because of this, healing comes more quickly than for those who deny and avoid grief. Even for children, ventilation and expression of grief must be allowed and encouraged in order that they may emerge a stronger, less fearful adult.

Further complications arise when there are multiple deaths. In one case, a mother and son of ten years were both killed in an automobile accident. The husband was at home with their eight year-old daughter when it happened. He was informed shortly afterwards by a police officer who came to the door. There was no one else at home. Unfortunately, the police officer proceeded to give a full account of the accident with the daughter present. At that point, the father was unable to speak and the child, focusing on his reaction took the lead from him and remained silent herself. All this when both father and child were inwardly screaming and shocked from the traumatic news they had just received. The police officer only then recognized their horror and offered to call relatives as well as seek support from the neighbors. At that point help was quickly brought in for the father and daughter.

How does one even begin to mourn when so much is lost? Here was a case where a man had lost his wife, his best friend, companion, but he had also lost his only son, the one who carried his genes, looked like him, was a beginning buddy and friend. It goes without saying, multiple losses carry with them the risk of poor bereavement outcome. So much is lost at one time that it is difficult to know how to focus on any one person, any one loss. It takes years to process and the pain is usually more intense than bereavements where attention can be placed on one person. However, where a child has died, it adds a further complication which affect parents in painful, unspeakable ways.

In the above case, there were several important variables working for the father and daughter. The family had been a close one, a farm family, where death was a familiar occurrence. They talked about their losses as they happened; a grandfather, an aunt, a beloved dog and many of the loved farm animals. The family mourned each loss sharing their feelings openly. Their little pet cemetery attested to the care that each beloved animal received.

Along with shared openness, they had a strong faith and belief in the full circle of life and death. Even so, theirs was not an easy grief; however, the father helped his daughter see that she was guiltless and most of all loved. She helped her father see that life still had some purpose and value and that he too was loved.

Parental Bereavement

When a child dies, the parents are left broken, empty and very much alone, different from every other person in the world. The wound cuts deeply and for some it never heals. It has been described as the most difficult, painful, and time-consuming loss anyone can survive.

What are the factors involved that create such a painful turbulence in bereaved parents?

The parent-child bond

The birth of a child represents a personal fulfillment for the parents. No other relationship in life is more important than the attachment they share. This attachment also tends to bring the parents closer to each other making them feel a part of each other through their child. When the child dies, the parents feel the loss as if they themselves had also died.

Identification

Parents not only share the same genes with their children but they also share a lazy part of life with them. The childhood years become a reliving of the parent's own childhood. Each developmental step represents a poignant memory of the parent's earlier life. The life of each parent is intertwined with the child and the future is anticipated not only in terms of what the child will accomplish but what the parent will accomplish through the child.

When a child dies, the parents grieve not only for the deprivation of being without their child but for the lost aspects of themselves as well.

Immortality

Children represent their parents' futures. Parents are unconsciously caught up in the lineage of their families and project themselves forward as they anticipate the future arrival of their children's children. When their child dies, parents feel robbed of their immortality, their futures stolen.

Social Agents

As the children grow, they become personal emissaries for the family. Much of family planning is centered around childhood activities. The child provides psychic energy which becomes the very fabric of family formation. When the child dies, the family has lost a large connection to other people or activities. The nest becomes empty before its time.

The Process of Grief

The process of grief is not a linear progression. They do not have clear-cut stopping and starting points but rather imply a free-flowing process. The bereavement process tends to fall into separate but over-lapping phases. As the bereaved individual moves through the phases toward renewal he is carried along often by biological as well as psychological symptoms. Symptoms of one phase often overlap the symptoms of the next. Or the individual may have a temporary regression into the previous phase. At the same time, it is important to remember that individuals react in characteristic ways. This does not preclude the phase. They remain to act as a general outline with the individual reactions working within each phase.

Understanding the general schema of the bereavement process allows one to have a better understanding of where they are going and what they will be experiencing. By having a benchmark the grieving individual can understand more fully what has been seen to effect others and in this knowledge, they become less fearful.

The Phases of Grief

Phase I-Shock

It is the shock reaction that creates such a long and difficult bereavement in parental grief. This phase, which usually passes after a few days to a week or two in most other losses, can last up to a year following the death of a child—in some cases even longer. Shock is a general term used to describe the amount of trauma that has been sustained. When a child dies, the disbelief, confusion, and helplessness place the parents in a state of physiological and emotional alarm. The world is no longer safe and the parents are caught up in the preoccupation of thoughts about their dead child.

As painful and chaotic as the shock phase is, it nevertheless provides an insulation against the terrible reality of their child's death. This does not mean there is no pain. Far from it. Still much of the agony is buffered until the parents can begin to cognitively process the event of death. Because of this, emotions are not fully realized yet.

As the protection of shock wears thin, the parents begin to realize the awful loneliness, the intense agony of being without their beloved child. The second phase has begun.

Awareness of Loss

The second phase of grief is one of intense emotional disorganization. The full awareness of their child's death feels like an unbearable weight. This is a phase when parents experience volatile emotions, anger, guilt, frustration and shame. They become more sensitive to what others say. The broken attachment feels like the sudden wrenching away of a part of their body. The world is unsafe. It is no longer predictable.

Again, for parental grief, this second phase of grief, just as it was for the first phase, lasts longer than for other types of loss. It is incomprehensible that their child could have been taken from them. Seemingly, they are left with nothing.

Conservation/Withdrawal

The exhaustive emotional discharge of the second phase wears heavily and at some point there is need for the bereaved parents to begin to conserve what little energy is left. This is not done consciously but is a result of the body and mind becoming thoroughly exhausted. There is nothing left to go on. They face an enforced rest that looks a great deal like depression but is instead a state of despair and hopelessness. This phase is a time of pulling back, ruminating, trying to come to grips with this awful tragedy that has befallen them. Yearning, bargaining, searching, all have failed. Now is a time of turning inward, of facing the loss, of realizing their child will never return. Hopelessness in this realization is the true meaning of despair. Yet, it is in this despair that resolution can finally take place. Life can never be the same as it was before.

In finally accepting this tragic condition, there is also the need to move on with their lives. This is the longest phase of all. For bereaved parents this may take years.

Although this phase is long and dismal, it is in the conserving of energy, the withdrawing from external activities, that bereaved individuals begin to regain some much needed energy. Because of this, they have the strength to reach a turning point in their grief. They are ready to move into the healing phase of grief.

Healing

This phase represents the turning point of grief. Healing comes slowly. However, as bereaved parents step out of the passive hibernation of phase three, there is now more energy to devote to healing. This phase is one of searching for meaning in the loss, an important task of parental bereavement. It is an important time of forgiving as well as forgetting (the tragic circumstances of the death, not the fulfilling times spent with the child before his death). Forgetting implies "letting go." Letting go of the past and looking toward the future. Perhaps the most difficult task is in closing the family circle—to join hands with the ones who are left and focus on living rather than on the dead child.

As parents find new ways of sharing life with each other and with the world outside themselves, the realization that they have changed and must also change many things about themselves becomes evident. The last phase of grief has pushed forward.

Renewal

Grief is akin to a death and resurrection experience. As part of oneself dies with the child, there is almost simultaneous preparation for a rebirth of the new self. Life will never be the same again. Learning to live without the precious child is one of the most difficult tasks of all. Yet, finding replacements for the energy that was once directed toward the child, can be an important part of becoming whole again. Biologically, the bereaved parents have had time to heal and renew their strength. The bereavement process continues as the grieving parents develop emotional stability. Special times such as anniversaries and holidays will still be painful and poignant, but the despair, helplessness and hopelessness of pain and longing that were once felt, have lifted.

Predicting how long it will take to move through the grieving process is impossible to determine. So much depends upon the relationship each parent had with the child, such as the situation in the family both before and after the death, the support of friends. Being willing to share the pain with others will be important in making the unreal real. Yet, nothing in grief is ever smooth and predictable. It takes time, patience, and a willingness to walk into the pain.

Marital problems

It has been estimated that 99 percent of all couples mourning the death of a child have some problems as a result of their child's death. However, it is difficult to estimate the percentage of dissolved marriages because so often the divorce or separation doesn't occur for several years following the child's death.

Most of the difficulty lies in the couple's perception that each partner will always be there to support the other one when feeling insecure. But grief is a singular process. Each person is alone and grieves in individual manners. When each parent is grieving differently, there is bound to be misunderstanding. A mother and father may not suffer the same loss when their child dies. Each had a separate and unique relationship and will grieve for different reasons. The father's grief may be diminishing while the mother's grief remains the same or grows more acute. Unless each partner is attuned to the other, this difference in grieving will be interpreted as another sign of either overemotional reacting or not caring enough. This is an important time for groups to be utilized for they offer an opportunity to balance emotions and hear the opposite viewpoint.

Gender Differences

Grief of fathers

Men and women have their separate roles in all cultures. These roles complement each other when things are going well. When things aren't going well, however, these separate roles act to make communication difficult. In our society, a man is socialized to take the following roles:

◆ Being strong
◆ Competing and winning
◆ Protecting the family and its possessions
◆ Being the family provider
◆ Being self-sufficient

When men are socialized to be strong, controlling, self-sufficient family protectors, the problem is that these characteristics work against open expression of emotions, grief included. Emotional displays are often seen as weaknesses. When a child dies, events are out of a father's control. Besides feeling an inner agony that he can't express, he feels powerless, stripped of the sense of self. He is angry and guilty, and has a strong sense of personal failure.

When the father remains woodenly stoic, trying to be all the things that are expected of him, he gives the impression of one who has no grief. When he doesn't want to talk about the child, the mother takes this as further indication that he simply doesn't care.

Yet, when caregivers continue to encourage fathers to talk about the dead child, about feelings that spring up during grief, not only the father but also the entire family will be helped to accept the reality of the death, while ensuring that no one is accused of forgetting the lost child or being unresponsive to grief.

A woman is socialized to fill a different role. She is expected to be:

◆ The nurturer
◆ The hub of the family
◆ Help each family member communicate with each other
◆ Carries the emotional burden of the family
◆ Creates the family circle

When a child dies, the circle is broken. Grief freezes the mother into a shell, and she cannot function in her prescribed roles as she once did. She grieves not only for her child, but also for the loss of the delicate balance in the family system.

Because she needs more nurturance for herself and is less able to give nurturance to others, she turns to her husband for help. But she often finds him withdrawn and unable to communicate. This is naturally seen as lack of love for the child and for herself as well. Because of greater sensitivity in grief than at any other time in life, the hurts are pushed down deeper and deeper. There is no way of dislodging or deflecting them.

Even sexual expression, which helped draw the couple together in the past, is impeded by the inability to trust or feel close now.

As a result, mothers find themselves locked in social isolation, not able to understand the full implication of what is taking place but having strong needs of their own that go unfulfilled.

What makes parental grief different from all other losses?

Despair

The reason parental grief is so different from other losses has to do with excess. Because loss of a child is such an unthinkable loss, everything is intensified, exaggerated, and lengthened. Guilt and anger are almost always present in every significant loss, but these emotions are inordinate with grieving parents. Experts estimate that it takes anywhere from three to five years to reach renewal after a spouse dies, but parental grief might go on for ten to twenty years or maybe a lifetime. Our lives are so severely altered when our child dies that there can be few replacements. The shock and severity of this kind of loss leaves parents feeling completely helpless and full of dark despair.

Confusion

When a child dies, the parents find it impossible to focus. Even the simplest of tasks is almost too much to figure out. There is a jumble of unintelligible thoughts as the mind races desperately to take in the horrible tragedy. Even light distractions such as watching TV no longer can offer the escape they used to.

Preoccupation with the dead child makes concentrating on anything impossible. Habitual tasks that used to be simple to perform, now take careful forethought. The bereaved parents simply can not slow their minds down long enough to quiet the confusion.

Anger

Anger has been among one of the severest reactions of bereaved parents. This is understandable when one considers the amount of helplessness generated by losing a beloved child. It pervades every thought and action. The very order of the universe has been altered. Because parents are responsible for their children and have acted as problem solvers and caregivers, when a child dies, parents are left with a sense of powerlessness. There is nothing to do to solve this problem. No matter what they do, they cannot bring their child back. The frustration is insurmountable and the awful deprivation leaves them with an intolerable rage but little on which to focus that rage.

Anger is a valuable means of giving expression to the powerlessness that is felt and is best dealt with by verbalization. Caregivers need to take a noncritical approach to accusations and outpourings of angry parents. Anger can be a facilitative emotional expression that, when encouraged in a positive and nonjudgmental manner, can help the bereaved parent to actively move through the emotional phase of grief without negative consequences.

Guilt

Guilt is a by-product of grief. One usually experiences guilt in almost all losses, however, with the death of a child, guilt becomes even more pronounced. Because parents feel responsible for their children, when something happens to them they immediately blame themselves. There is a feeling that they should have been taking better care of them, that they should have been there to prevent such a horrible accident from happening.

Survivor guilt is another form of guilt that plagues bereaved parents. This form of guilt comes from the firm expectation that our children will naturally survive us. Thus the continuation of the species is ensured. When this pattern is broken, when the parent survives the child, the parent feels tremendous guilt and shame.

Guilt, like anger, is best dealt with by talking it over with a trusted friend or professional. Letting go of guilt takes courage in that one must confess some privately held thoughts. Yet, it is in doing just that that one can be emancipated from the torment that accompanies long-lasting guilt reaction.

Unresolved Grief

The reasons for the severe reactions in child loss have been addressed earlier: the strong bond between parents and child, the sense of responsibility that parents have for caring for their child, the guilt and shame survivors inevitably live with, the parents' belief that they have failed, their lost future, and the parents' identification with the child. When parents lose a child they lose a large part of themselves. Resolving all these issues takes an enormous amount of time and energy—and pain. Resolving the loss of a child is a slow, hard process, harder and slower than any other type of bereavement. Here are some types of grief that have the potential for being unresolved; inhibited or suppressed grief; unsupported grief; and chronic grief.

Inhibited Grief

Resolution requires one to learn to live without. One must give up the beloved child but also the many facets of the relationship such as the role of mother or father, the love object and source of love that the child provided. Before grief can be resolved, parents must let go of the emotional involvements they had with their dead child. This is an extremely difficult task for any parent to accomplish. For some it is impossible.

Resolution of grief means that one must acknowledge the reality of death. This means experiencing the pain of grief. Some parents try to avoid this task by denying the event of death, by hanging on to hopeless hope. Yet, embracing the pain, going toward it and through it, is the only way to come out the other side. The pain is what finally heals one.

Unsupported Grief

Social support is one of the primary aids in adequately resolving a major loss. When support is plentifully provided, when the loss can be shared with the community, it appears that bereavement can be eased and its length shortened. However, when a loss must be suffered alone, when the community shuns the griever, then alienation and shame are heaped upon that individual and there is no longer a connection with the world. It is as if that individual had has been banished much like certain tribal members when a member was cast outside the community to die. Without support from others during this most tragic of circumstances, bereaved parents feel their own personal "death" as well as the death of their child. The following represent a list of unsupported grievers in our own society. They are parents of:

◆ Murdered children
◆ Suicides
◆ Missing children
◆ MIAs
◆ Single parents
◆ New to the community
◆ Miscarriage
◆ Abortions
◆ Relinquishing child for adoption

Unsupported grief sentences bereaved parents to untold suffering. Having a caring and nurturing individual near reduces the pain and undue suffering. Beyond that it paves the way for that grieving person to move toward the resolution of bereavement and allows him to carry on the support to someone else who needs it.

Chronic Grief

There are many cases where a bereaved parent refuses to relinquish her grief and instead carries on as if nothing had changed. It is as if the child was away at camp or school and she has everything in order for his return. Not letting go of one's grief means staying in a perpetual state of denial. One must let go of emotional involvements with the dead child in order to resolve the pain and move on to a renewed place in life.

Searching for Meaning

When a child has died, the question of meaning is always there in the back of parents' minds. The constant "Why?" in the beginning is part of this. They are plagued by the need to find an answer that could explain this enormous tragedy. Each parent asks "How could God allow my child to die and leave me here? What good am I? What is the meaning of life now that everything has changed?" These questions cannot be answered easily or quickly.

Not until the bereaved parent has gained some distance from the shock of loss, worked through the realization and acknowledgement of the death, and begun to accept the inevitable changes occurring can he start to answer questions concerning the meaning of life. As one experiences greater spiritual strength, one gains a greater acceptance of ones own competency in dealing with a need for direction. Then, as these directions begin to lead to places where one can find satisfactions while renewing confidence, faith in the world slowly begins to return.

References

Fitzgerald, H. *The Grieving Child: A Parent's Guide*, Simon & Schuster: New York, 1992.

Grollman, E. *Talking About Death: A Dialogue Between Parent and Child*, Boston: Beacon Press, 1970.

LeShan, E. *Learning to Say Good-by When a Parent Dies*, Avon, New York, 1978.

Rando, T. *Parental Loss of a Child*, Research Press Co., Champaign, IL, 1986.

Raphael, B. *The Anatomy of Bereavement*, Hutchinson, London, 1984.

Sanders, C. *How to Survive the Loss of a Child*, Prima Publishing, 1992.

Sanders, C. *Surviving Grief and Learning to Live Again*, John Wiley & Sons, New York, 1992.

Stroebe, M., Stroebe, W., and Hansson, R. Handbook of Bereavement: Theory, Research, and Intervention, 1993.

Children and Traumatic Loss 7

Ronald K. Barrett

A n eight year old boy is shot in a playground, an accidental victim of a "drive by" shooting. Three young girls are killed on their way to school as an out of control car careens into a sidewalk. A tornado rips through a suburban school crashing down a cafeteria wall, fatally injuring children as they eat lunch.

All of these vignettes, captured by recent headlines, remind us, that like adults, children may experience losses that are both sudden and traumatic. Indeed, the very nature of contemporary society, plagued by violence, has placed this generation of children in the United States at a level and kind of unprecedented risk.

And in children this risk may be especially complicated. For many of the same trends that beget the violence, such as the epidemic of drug use, also impair the child's ability to find effective support.

For the grief recovery and subsequent emotional and mental health of children is critically and primarily dependent upon the social support available through parent caregivers in the home. With the number of relevant losses in that primary support system of children—dysfunctional caregivers, breakdown of families—as well as increasing dysfunction of traditional child welfare and protection institutions, children are increasingly at risk.

The child's survival challenge is further compounded by divorce and separation from the extended family, by drug and alcohol abuse, domestic violence, gang and community violence, and the HIV/ AIDS epidemic. Understandably many children have lost the sense of safety and innocence romantically characterized as childhood. In many communities, it is increasingly apparent that we ought to regard children as "secondary victims" of chronic community violence since children who witness violence are at risk of trauma that may have fairly long-term consequences.

Indeed, an emerging body of research on Post-Traumatic Stress Disorder (PTSD) forecasts difficulties for an increasing number of American children who experience traumatic and violent loss. In general the behavioral symptoms may include severe depression, emotional regression and/or the avoidance of affect (e.g. the appearance, and possibly the reality, of being insensitive, uncaring, and without feelings). The consequences of grief associated with a significant loss and PTSD can intensely manifest itself in male children in expressions of anger that resembles rage. Female children who are securely socialized and sex-typed as feminine more typically turn their anger inward and consequently are less likely to demonstrate the intensity of anger seen in male children.

Grieving children grieve intermittently and are more inclined to show signs of emotional instability as any number of trigger events cause a relapse into grieving and mourning. Typically children experiencing trauma, grief and loss may manifest varying degrees of mental preoccupation with grief work characterized by absent-mindedness, forgetfulness, accident proneness and ultimately a decline in academic performance. In addition the appearance of attention-seeking behaviors and a regression to clinging behaviors are common behavioral manifestations in the classroom. While many factors (e.g. the type of cause of death, the quality of the child's relationship to the deceased, the level of trauma via direct witness and exposure to the death, the extent of social stigma, etc.) may impact on the grief of the child. The provision of social support by parental figures is a critical factor in the grieving child's recovery.

Parents, as we know from experience and the literature, are the primary social support for children as their influence on the developing child is unrivaled by other support in the child's life. For the grieving child, witness to the violent or traumatic loss, burdened with anxiety and distress, few others can provide the quality of social and emotional support of the parent. In addition to providing comfort, social support, and reassurance of safety, parents also can provide a critical function as role models of how to grieve.

This discussion, then, suggests a number of critical conclusions. First, traumatic loss creates particular difficulties since it in itself assaults the sense of assumed safety that many persons including children need as they live. The "assumed reality" that one could go about normal business, such as walking to the store, is deeply challenged if one sees another child hit by a car or shot doing the same task. Even everyday events then seem unsettled and unsafe.

This sense of trauma is compounded when parents are themselves the victim of traumatic loss or are unavailable to the traumatized child. Since the child may be unaware of the extent of his or her own trauma, or unable to address it, caregivers need to be sensitive to many manifestations such as changes in academic performance, nightmares, acting out or regressive behaviors, or other manifestations of grief.

Traumatic loss too may be compounded when it is multiple. Children who experience multiple losses, especially traumatic ones, even in a serial fashion, are more at risk for complicated grief reactions. In such cases, parents may wish to consider professional assistance. Resolving traumatic loss is complicated since it involves dealing both with the trauma *and* loss. Parents, when possible, need to be a primary support, but they do not need to be the only assistance that the child receives.

Recommendations for Parents and Caregivers

1. It is important that parents accept their role and responsibility as primary support for children—especially children experiencing trauma, grief, and loss.
2. Parents should try to learn as much as they can about grief and mourning and just be available as a source of support to children. It is important that the child knows a parent cares and is reassured that the parent is there for them. Where that is absent, the potential for serious problems inevitably exists.
3. A holistic intervention plan involving all the important support for children is most effective and can potentially maximize the therapeutic benefits for children in grief and mourning. For example, teachers and youth workers are also critical support in the lives of children. A multifocused intervention involving the home, school, and community can be most beneficial.
4. The children's grief support groups are recommended as having the best therapeutic outcome for children especially when they combine individual counseling and creative art therapies (i.e. bibliotherapy, art therapy, puppets, movement therapy, etc.). These expressive therapies can be especially helpful in clinical interventions with children.
5. Individual differences should be respected. Each child may grieve differently. Sensitivity to differences in culture, age, gender, and the type of loss must be recognized.
6. For all individuals involved in the support of children in grief

and mourning it is important to be diligent in resolving their own issues regarding loss to be able to assist rather than encumber children in their grief recovery.

7. As adults we must not be in denial of death, our fears and anxiety, grief nor hide our mourning from children. It is healthier that adults honestly share themselves with children as a way to teach that loss and grief are a part of life. This fundamental lesson in death education with children can be shared during opportunistic events such as the death of a pet or other living creatures.

8. The trauma of a significant loss for a child takes time and requires patience and understanding especially from significant adults (e.g. parents, teachers, guardians, youth workers, etc.) All should be informed of the child's experience.

9. Funerals are important rituals and events for the release of grief via mourning. Funerals are also a valuable occasion for death education for children to observe and learn much about their religion and cultural heritage. Children should be told what to expect at funerals and given choices (to attend or not attend, view or not to view, etc.)

Finally, despite all of the pitfalls, children are not as fragile as they are resilient. With some help and lots of support, most do recover—one day at a time.

How Can We Help

8

Stephen P. Hersh

This discussion focuses on the span of childhood from ages 2 years through age 12 years. Some of the principles and recommendations presented have relevance to both infants and adolescents but their responses to loss as well as their ways of grieving are different. Infants and adolescents' reactions to death warrant being addressed separately.

Principles

Remember the "peek-a-boo" game with infants and toddlers? The behaviors of these very young children during that game reminds all of us that separation, starting with something so basic as disappearance from sight, has powerful effects on the behaviors and moods of even the very young. As children become older those effects become more complex as well as more powerful. Separation from a cared for and/or needed person produces anxiety in all humans. Our introduction to needing the contact and closeness of someone, which becomes the basis for our caring, loving and being cared for, begins in infancy as does our introduction to the discomfort and uncomfortable state of hyper-alertness that we call anxiety. The sight, smell, warmth of being held and pleasure of being fed or rocked by that needed presence quiets down any feelings and behaviors expressing distress. Learning as infants that our noises of distress bring to us the comforting caretaker on a predictable basis lays the foundation for an expectation we call "basic trust" and a state of mind called hopefulness: that comfort is attainable through our actions and expressions of feelings.

Those early experiences when reasonably reinforcing of basic trust allow all of us to cope with the separation experiences we encounter in normal growth and development — the parent is not always around and available; going to new places; encountering other adults and other children; going to pre-school, etc. For most people in our culture those early experiences reinforce an expectation, which eventually becomes a belief, that changes as well as disappearances are reversible. Only with increasing experience and age, usually not before 7 years, do children begin to understand that changes may not be reversible, including "disappearances" of fond objects, pets, or people through all the different ways that things, pets and people can disappear. The awareness that disappearance or loss or death is not reversible generates a higher level of anxiety around the experience of separation, particularly through death, because separation is now paired with *loss of control* — the discovery that no matter what you wish, who you ask, or what you do, you can not un-make the loss; the separation from the loved and cared for person is the way it is!

When you help children, remember the many ways they differ from one another. First, as implied in the above comments, children of different ages experience loss, separation anxiety, and the feelings that accompany these experiences very differently. The average three year old is quite different in his or her perceptions of and reactions to loss from the average seven, or nine, or eleven year old. *In addition, children of the same age are not necessarily of the same developmental and emotional level of development.* For this reason do your best to learn about the particular child you are trying to help as the individual he or she actually is.

As children age their world of interaction with others expands. Different children will therefore have very different experiences in both number and kind with separation or loss or death — from moves, to leaving friends, to travel, to loss of pets, to loss of grandparents or siblings or a parent. In helping a child deal with a loss learn first about what other experiences with loss the child has suffered.

Remind yourself that the sense of time children experience differs significantly from that of adults. (Think back simply to how long summertime once seemed to you as a child and how quickly it goes now in your adult years.) When helping children with death, refer to the ceremonies surrounding death and after death using time in ways that are meaningful to them. For young children the references are meal times, getting-up times, story or play times and going-to-bed time. Hours on the clock or days on the calendar are relatively meaningless.

Children deal with and digest feelings through play and through fantasy. To notice that a five-year old, for example, after being told that his mother or father died, quietly wanders off to his room and starts to play with his toys is to notice appropriate coping behavior. Understand it for what it is, being open to the child returning to ask questions, rather than finding it a strange or unemotional response to the news. The child's response is neither strange nor unemotional, it is just not an adult's response. Along the same lines, when a child is told something the child may nod his or her head to indicate understanding. We accept this gesture with fellow adults and assume — not always correctly — that they understood what we told them the way we wanted them to understand it. It is not unreasonable for us to expect this when helping adults.

With children *never* interpret a head nod when you are explaining something to them as you would with an adult. They have learned the gesture from adults, but frequently it is for the child simply the easiest way to get the "helping" adult to leave them alone. If it is critical that you verify the understanding of a child who is nodding his or her head that they understand, always gently ask the child to tell you what they just heard and to explain it to you in their own words.

Bereavement for children, as for all of us, is influenced by many factors. These include who died, the age and relationship of the person with respect to oneself (a playmate, parent, sibling, grandparent, family friend), whether or not the child was present at the death, whether or not the death was anticipated or sudden, whether it was violent or non-violent, and even if non-violent did the deceased suffer in dying and were they disfigured by their particular death. All these factors will influence the feelings and behaviors of the children. They will interact with the child's previous experiences, the understanding as influenced by age and developmental stage, the reactions of family members around them, behaviors of peers, and finally by how the entire experience of death is organized and dealt with in the context of the child's particular family's culture and its traditions.

How to Help

1. When a child has caring, involved parent(s), the parents are key. Respect the parents, finding out their wishes, needs and expectations of the child during this time of loss. Most parents when

approached in this fashion share their traditions and expectations, and are open to assistance as well as suggestions.

2. In the context of the above, ideally involved clergy, family members, health care providers and teachers should work together, allowing themselves to be orchestrated by the parent(s). Who died, the nature of the death, and the ceremonies mandated by cultural and religious traditions will influence the appropriate timing of the different types of help.

3. Do not try to fix anything. Death, loss, bereavement are realities that differ from the specific event of dying. They are realities of the living; as such they take enormous amounts of time to become real for the sufferers as well as to be folded into the realities of the every day feelings, events and behaviors of all of us. This is just such a powerful reality for children. They will, unlike adults, because they are growing and developing rapidly, more intensely re-digest the loss as they move to new stages of social and emotional and cognitive awareness.

4. Following from the above, do not impose adult expectations about *responses and emotional expressions* to the ceremonies around the deceased or commemorating the deceased. But, do involve children in those ceremonies while guiding them in appropriate behaviors while there. Tell them that they can ask questions, ask them if they have questions, and "listen" to them — not infrequently a comment has within it a request for help in understanding. The balance is between listening and not over-explaining.

5. Be patient in your helping and be accepting of differences. Children even within the same family and even when close in age have very different personalities. As the helping adults you may be more comfortable with a highly verbal child but that verbal expressiveness in and of itself does not necessarily say anything about that particular child's coping nor does the perhaps less attractive silence of his sibling necessarily mean that the quiet sibling should be of greater concern.

6. The ceremonies for the deceased as well as the memorials are positive organizing experiences for the survivors. Children should attend them. They, whenever possible if the deceased is a parent, sibling, grandparent or peer, should be helped to participate in the ceremony in some appropriate way.

7. Allow particularly young children to engage in play. Encourage them to draw and to tell stories; let stories with loss, bereavement and "re-constitution of life after loss" themes be read to them. As mentioned earlier these are the ways that children over time "work through," integrate and make some sense out of the separation and loss of control that death brings.

8. For the older, school age child, help him or her with her peer group. Learn from the child what he or she is saying, if anything, to peers about the death of the loved one. Listen and learn from the child what the responses are to this information from peers. Here is one frequent place for adult modulation, explanation, comforting, and intervening since few in our culture have experience with death. As a result the responses of peers and their parents can be awkward, even unhelpful. In some schools and with some children, parent and teacher might chose to work together to help the child make known his or her loss to the class group in a way that encourages their support while providing some education and sensitization of peers about death. (I do *not* recommend school guidance counselor-led support groups for children in this age range. Such groups do exist in an increasing number of the high schools around the country. For teenagers, less controlled by parents and family, school counselor-led groups apparently serve a useful purpose.)

9. Children are excellent and sensitive observers. It is hard to fool them about feelings in particular. They will observe the behaviors especially of the adults around them. If there are examples of dramatic behaviors (expressive or withdrawal), explain them to the child briefly and do so in words appropriate for the child's developmental stage. Explain also tears, fatigue, irritability, especially your own. Such explaining comforts the child; it also helps the child to accept (as children naturally want to do) the naturalness of feelings as well as the legitimacy of expressing them.

10. Once past the ceremonies, the memorial services, ordinary reality takes over. Memories go up and down in intensity; confusion about time may occur. Anxiety may develop about forgetting. Here you can help the child in many ways. If, particularly, the pre-school or early school age child starts to ask questions or talk in ways that fly in the face of your adult per-

ceptions that death, a permanent loss of presence, has occurred, do not challenge the child. Listen. Learn more by asking questions about play observed by you, drawings, questions posed by the child. Re-explain events and then begin a process of helping the child to organize his or her memories. This involves talk, mementos, pictures, visits perhaps to a gravesite. This is all a process to be repeated over and over as months and as years go by. The process has some intense moments separated as time passes by first days, then weeks, then months, then years.

11. Encourage learning about how to live with death and loss. Children, just as adults, need help in maintaining the courage to face their feelings of sadness, of anger, of helplessness. Children, as adults, need help in regaining after a major loss through death, their sense of hope. Learning about the experiences of others helps immensely over time. Many children, and surviving parents, find, for example, the photojournalist Jill Krementz' book *How It Feels When a Parent Dies* very helpful. It is composed of 18 interviews and photographs of children age 7 through 16 years talking about their feelings and reactions to the death of a parent. (Alfred A. Knopf, New York 1986)

12. Finally, when is professional help needed for children who have experienced death? In most situations children do not need professional help individually or in groups. For the usual kinds of death from age or illness (any age) children cope, grow and develop quite well with a loving, caring family, friends, community (including church or synagogue or temple) who follow common sense as well as the precepts listed above.

However, there are situations in which children always need the assistance of a well-trained, family-oriented mental health professional. When death occurs through violence, whether that violence be natural or "man-made," professional consultation is always warranted. Depending upon the circumstances, intervention by individuals or teams of professionals, working with the children and families involved, helps significantly to deal not only with the immediate fears and symptoms (e.g. nightmares, loss of appetite, inability to go out into the community, increased and inappropriate aggressive behaviors, etc.), but also to prevent long term consequences that can be placed under the broad category of Post Traumatic Stress Disorders. Such violence can, of course, be from massive flooding, tornados, earthquakes and hurricanes. Man-made violence can range from individual attacks to group or mob violence to the constant violence experienced in riot or war zones. None of these experiences is easy for the average person in the natural order of things. For children, these events are as fearful and confusing as for adults. But, more disorienting and disturbing for children is their experiencing simultaneously with the events, the extreme anxiety and fear of the adults who are supposed to be comforting and taking care of them. The natural dependency and sensitivity of children to others amplifies tremendously their emotional reactions while the relative incapacitation or impotence of involved adults undermines whatever psychological defenses a child might have that are appropriate to his age.

Unfortunately, not all children come from well-functioning two-parent or single-parent families or from family systems in which their caretakers see their development as a priority. For the many forms of disrupted and dysfunctional family systems children are left to deal with death and bereavement without structure, without consistent support, without explanation, comfort or understanding. This is where there is the greatest need for appropriate members of the community, congregation, health care system and school system to work together on behalf of the child. Which of the helping disciplines takes the primary goal must be determined by the availability of help, matched as closely as possible to the nature and intensity of the needs revealed by the individual child.

The Role of the School: 9
Bereaved Students & Students Facing Life-Threatening Illness

Robert G. Stevenson

In an effort to provide our children with a "better life," we have come to rely heavily on our schools. The people of this country believe strongly that education must be available to every child. To reach this goal we have created a system which offers *universal* public education. The public schools of America have been given a mandate to educate the *whole child*. Every child is unique, a special and precious individual. Every child comes to our schools with special needs. Some of these needs require special care and attention. These physical, emotional or cognitive needs are increasingly addressed by caring, well-trained professionals.

It is easy for most people to see that a student battling a life-threatening illness clearly has special needs. Bereaved children and adolescents are also students with special needs, as are the classmates of each of these students. However, to really help these young people, we need to *know* what these students needs are and to *understand* how these needs can best be addressed. We must determine what role, if any, a school can play in this effort. Finally, parents, educators and caring members of the community-at-large must work together to establish policies and procedures which can be implemented to help these students address their special needs.

Bereaved Students

Death touches the lives of young people far more frequently than most of us would like to admit. Robert Kastenbaum has called childhood "the kingdom where nobody dies," but even in the lives of the most protected children, death is a dark intruder in that "perfect" fantasy world. One child in twenty will have a parent die before they graduate from high school, most often the father. In an elementary school, each death of a parent touches every child who hears of it, triggering fear that a similar fate could befall someone in that child's life. A high school teacher must be aware that it is quite likely that one or more of the students in every class they teach has suffered the death of a parent. These deaths have an impact on the learning process and should be the subject of ongoing dialogue between teachers and parents. However, parents may not contact teachers because of a belief that schools have planned for such tragic circumstances; that educators will know what to do. Some parents may remain silent because they feel that this loss is a family matter and that the school has no role to play. Teachers themselves may be reluctant to say or do anything, afraid that whatever they do or say may be wrong or even harmful. School personnel may be reluctant to "intrude" on a family's grief, not sure what they can say or do to help. As adults, our uncertainty or misunderstanding may cause us confusion or anxiety, but the ones who are really hurt are our children. When the important adults in a child's life do not react to a death, when they fail to answer a child's questions, it can cause confusion, anger and even guilt in the children the adults seek to protect.

Recommendation #1: Parents and teachers must establish and maintain ties so that each can inform the other about important developments in a child's life as they occur. This ongoing communication can be invaluable in helping bereaved students of all ages.
Young children have many questions about dying, death and the feelings they experience in connection to these events. Death can claim grandparents, parents, siblings, peers, or neighbors. The death of a classmate, teacher or administrator can have an impact on every child in a school. Through the media, a single death can touch the lives of tens of thousands of children. Even the death of an animal can have a major impact on a child.

Most children love without reservation. If there are no limits on their love, why should we think that they can place limits on their pain when the object of that love is gone? That "object" is typically thought to be a person, but it might be an item connected to a person, one that represents the bond between the child and the person (a keepsake given to them by a now-deceased loved one), or it might be a pet. We adults sometimes try to limit the pain of a child's loss by saying the relationship was not that important to the child ("It was only a dog or cat."). Not only do comments like this fail in their purpose, they can convince a child that the adult who is trying to help really has no idea what this loss means or how it has hurt them.

It is also true that young children believe the present can remain unchanged. They feel their wishes can come true. How are these children to understand death? It can shatter their view of the world as a safe, unchanging place. If things only happen when they wish them, what role did they play in causing/allowing this death? Death is on television and in movies. They see it in reality in nature, whether it is seen in the cycle of the seasons, or in the form of a dead squirrel in the road. The unspoken role that children feel in a death of a person or a pet, if not addressed, can be the start of a lifetime of concealed guilt. This death can be the first in a series of losses with which the child seeks to cope through denial or avoidance.

The way a young person views death changes as the child grows and develops. A child is at birth "ignorant" about death and moves through several stages in coming to an adult understanding of it. Most pre-school children and some students, up to second or third grade, see death as temporary or reversible. When the deceased does not return, they can be filled with anger or guilt (believing they are the reason the deceased loved one does not come back). Children from third grade to fifth grade and older (in some cases even as old as high school students) view death as a person, place or thing. This belief gives them hope that they can avoid this death "place" or "person" and that they and their loved ones need not die. To avoid the many complications that can occur due to ignorance, or misunderstanding, children need accurate knowledge about death. The earlier they have this foundation upon which to build, the stronger they will be when forced to face the losses every life, and death, brings.

Recommendation #2: There is some information about death which is essential for all young people to know, regardless of cultural difference or religious beliefs.

If we are to help young people keep the pain of a loss from becoming even greater because of misunderstanding there are three basic concepts which they must learn. Children must learn that a dead body deceased no longer experiences anything. They cannot feel hot or cold or pain ever again. This physical reality of death lasts forever. Unlike movies or television, in the real world death is permanent and irreversible. Finally, they need to know that all living things die. Death is universal. There are many excellent books which treat these facts in a clear and age appropriate way for young pre-schoolers through the complex fantasy life of the adolescent.

Grieving students show their reactions to the death of a loved one in many ways. The following list is by no means comprehensive, and we must remember that individual students may not exhibit all of these reactions. However, each of these can cause pain and confusion for the student and may be misunderstood by those who care about this young person. A student's grief may be exhibited through:

◆ **poor academic performance** — The changes connected to a death produce stress and the fear of future deaths can cause anxiety. Both fear and anxiety can impair the academic performance of students. Coping with grief requires energy and concentration and there may not be much left for schoolwork. Even an increased effort in school may not yield the usual results. This can add to the students feelings of confusion and, especially in cases where the deceased took pride in the student's school accomplishments, guilt.

◆ **apathy** — Apathy can be defined as "withdrawal from life." Bereaved students may not be able to enjoy the life that has been taken from their relative or friend. They may still attend activities that they formerly enjoyed, but the zest, the fun seems to be gone.

◆ **punishment seeking behavior** — Students may seek punishment from school authorities (as well as from family members at home) as a means of coping with extreme feelings of anger or guilt. Fighting, already becoming more common among students of all ages, may be triggered by feelings of anger which the students experiences but cannot pin on one particular person or thing. Some students may even punish themselves with recurring "accident" causing self-injury. Any pattern of violence or self-injury as a way of dealing with grief should be a cause of immediate concern. Left alone, perhaps by adults who do not wish to complicate their earlier loss, such a coping pattern can escalate. Students may even begin to pursue "risk-taking" behavior as a way of reasserting control over life. All of these behaviors can create a pattern which might lead to serious injury or even death. Drinking alcohol or using drugs, often seen by parents and teachers as a problem in themselves, may actually be an attempt by a young person at "self-medication" in an attempt to deal with unresolved grief. The substance abuse, if treated in isolation, will probably reoccur if the grief-related issues are not addressed.

◆ **changes in values** — Some students may decide that the quality of life is more important than its quantity. They may start to question every direction to determine what this means to them or to their lives. They may also move to the other extreme and question nothing, having decided that life no longer has value or meaning.

◆ **asking questions or spreading rumors** — A death can make that part of a student's life seem to be "out of control." Students may try to balance things by gaining a greater feeling of control in other areas. If the questions are not answered (even when they seem to be "off the topic") it can trigger the release of pent-up anger. Rumors must be addressed, but the students who spread such rumors must be helped to see the possible consequences of their actions. Punishment alone will not usually accomplish this.

◆ **the use of humor** — Such "humor" may appear inappropriate or tasteless. It is good to remember that we often "joke" about the things we fear. Just look at the way in which people seek to use humor after some catastrophe (i.e. the Challenger explosion, the death of JFK, even a group suicide by unhappy adolescents). Such humor helps the person to feel some control in the aftermath of the event. If we can laugh at it, the laughter can help release nervous tension and can help the student to feel less frightened. It may even be an attempt by students to distance themselves, and their friends, from such an event in the future. The danger here is that such jokes or stories can cause harm, usually unintentional, to others. When the student who told the jokes becomes aware of the pain caused by their actions, it can aggravate feelings of guilt. Inappropriate humor may also be a cry for help. One girl told the same story about the explosion of the Challenger over and over, even though her mother and her teacher asked her to stop. When she did not, her mother even punished her by sending her to her room. It was only after her mother heard her daughter screaming in her sleep one night and asked her about her nightmare that the cause of both the nightmare and the "jokes" became clear. If someone had taken the time to ask why she continued to tell that joke, the young girl might have received help sooner.

It is important to remember that these behaviors linked to the grief of a young person may not be shown for several years. A delay of the experience of grief for up to five years is not unusual. If a student in eleventh grade is experiencing a delayed grief reaction to the death of a parent which took place in sixth grade, it may well be misunderstood. The student has a drop in grades, loses interest in school sports and activities, argues with teachers and friends parents and teachers will most likely look for a reason. If that student is found to be drinking or taking drugs, that is where the search for answers ends...it is the drugs. Actually, in the case of unresolved grief it is not the drugs.

They are just one more symptom of the problem grieving. Educators and parents need to understand both the grief process and the different time frame that the grief of young people may follow.

Recommendation #3 — If there are students every year who must learn to cope with the death of a relative or friend, schools should have protocols in place to use when such events occur.

A set of guidelines for developing a protocol for a school's response to community grief was distributed in 1986 by the National Association of Secondary School Principals (Stevenson/Powers, 1986). The protocol was developed in response to concerns voiced by students about the way in which the explosion of the Challenger Space Shuttle was dealt with (or *not* dealt with) in their school. It includes a set of rules for informing an individual of a death, a task which is more and more common in schools.

Guidelines for Informing an Individual of a Loss

Who should inform the student?

◆ The student should be told by someone he/she sees as an *authority figure.* Administrators normally take on this task, but guidance personnel, a school nurse, or a classroom teacher may also carry out this task.

- Someone who has a *close relationship* with the student (teacher, nurse, counselor, or fellow student) should be with the student and should be able to remain after the student receives the news.

Where should the student be told?

- The student should be taken to a place where he/she can have *privacy*.
- The student should be able to sit or to lie down if necessary. A school nurse's office can fulfill both requirements.

How should the student be told?

- The student should be told what has happened in a quiet, simple and direct manner.
- Platitudes or religious symbolism should be avoided.
- The child's questions should be answered openly and honestly but unnecessary details need not be volunteered.
- Emotions and feelings should not be avoided.
- The wishes of the family, if they are known, should be respected as much as possible.

How will a student react?

- After a student has received the news, he or she may have any of a number of possible reactions. Educators must remember that there is no one "correct" response.
- The student should not be left alone.
- If the student remains silent, inform him/her that it is all right to speak about feelings.
- It is essential that staff reaction to a student not appear judgmental.

Who else should be informed?

- The family should be aware of what the student was told and all of the child's teachers, the school nurse, and school counselors should be informed of the situation as soon as possible.

The protocol was based on questions which must be answered when a school is faced with dealing with widespread grief, often referred to as "community" grief.

Guidelines For Informing Groups of Students

Where should the students be told?

◆ Large group presentations are almost always less beneficial for individual students. Whenever possible, students should receive the news of a crisis situation in familiar surroundings with people they know and trust. The classroom offers such a setting.

How should the students be told?

◆ Preselected staff members will be sent to inform all students of the event(s) that has occurred.
◆ Not every educator will be comfortable performing such a task and this must be determined in advance.
◆ A team of educators (called a "crisis response team" in some districts) should receive additional training concerning student needs in times of grief and/or stress.
◆ The same information should be given to all students.
◆ The information should be given in a calm, direct inner and the team members should stay to assist the classroom teacher in answering questions and addressing feelings and reactions.
◆ The nurse should not be among those staff members sent to inform students since some students may experience physical distress or have specific somatic complaints and will need the nurse to be available to perform her primary task as a medical professional.

How will the students react?

◆ While it is difficult to predict the reaction of an individual student, the reaction of *groups* of students is predictable.
◆ Students may feel sad or angry and will express these feelings.
◆ Students may feel guilty and seek to withdraw from interaction with peers or teachers.
◆ Students may not appear to feel anything at all. Some students may actually not be affected by the news or feel any personal involvement. However, there are students who *appear* uninvolved but are actually seeking to mask thoughts or feelings with which they are uncomfortable.
◆ It is essential that students be helped to understand that virtually

all of these reactions are "normal" because, however the individual student reacts, it is a response others share.

◆ The intensity of individual reactions may be a cause for concern. A school protocol must provide assistance for those students who need individual support.

◆ Training and workshops should be provided for counselors, social workers, school nurses and interested teachers on a regular basis.

Who else should be informed?

◆ All staff members must be kept informed of the details of events related to this death.

◆ Parents must be kept informed of the actions taken in school and of the events which affect their children.

◆ All communication must be two-way. School officials and teachers must solicit and be responsive to input from parents about their children.

What issues can complicate student reaction and/or school response?

◆ Certain events have been found to be factors which may produce complicated student reactions in times of crisis. The type of death can produce a grief reaction which is different from that which follows a death caused by illness or accident (Stevenson, 1994)

Recommendation #4 — Teachers need to be aware of specific actions they can take to aid bereaved students.

There are some steps which every teacher can take to help bereaved students. With younger students teachers should:

◆ make an effort to provide the student with a secure and safe environment.

◆ follow a schedule which reflects the "normal" routine as closely as possible. Bereaved children do not need the stress of more changes.

◆ allow, and be alert for, questions which relate to the child's loss.

◆ present some lessons which allow for discussion of the topic of death or loss. Children's literature provides numerous books which can be used.

- ◆ understand that the child may have a greater need for attention.
- ◆ adjust testing schedules and postpone standardized tests whenever possible. One principal gave a standardized test one week after the death of a student. The results for almost all students were predictably a disaster, one which could have been avoided.
- ◆ be watchful for changes in the student's behavior or classwork (art, writing, etc.) that may indicate the need for special support. If the child has trouble concentrating, which may occur after a death, allow the child to visit another place in the school, to take a "break." The school nurse's office is ideal for such a respite.
- ◆ keep lines of communication open with parents and guidance personnel.
- ◆ be careful about touching the student. It was once recommended that a hand on the shoulder, or a hug for a young child, could help calm an emotionally upset youngster. However, because even the most innocent contact may be misinterpreted, it is now suggested that most touching be avoided.

Recommendation #5 — Death education programs should be in place as part of a preventive approach to grief-related problems in older students.

Death education is that formal instruction which deals with dying, death, grief, loss and their impact on the individual and humankind. (Stevenson, 1984) These courses assist students by presenting facts about the physical aspects of death, the psychosocial effects of death on the survivors, and methods of coping with dying, death and grief. In a school setting, death education includes those courses, curricula, counseling programs and support services which offer a structured approach to issues dealing with dying, death, grief, loss and their impact on the students, staff, their families, their friends and on society.

After a quarter century of death education in our schools, the need for such courses and programs is clearer than ever. Although some would like to cling to the illusion that death does not touch the lives of adolescents, the reality is quite different. One in every 750 young people of high school age dies each year. Each of those deaths affects not just the students at one school, but at schools throughout the area. One in 20 young people will lose a parent to death by their senior year in high school (Critelli, 1979). Sibling deaths, celebrity deaths (of adolescents' "heroes" or cult figures), and staff deaths (as the average age of school faculty grows older) also affect high school age adolescents. Potentially, there are students trying to cope with their grief in every class in every school in this country. Thus, the difference among adolescents is not whether or not they have been affected by grief. They differ in their degree of success in coping with that grief.

Grief can have a dramatic impact on the classroom atmosphere and on the learning process. As with younger children, grief can affect a student in a number of ways:

- **academic** — a shorter attention span, difficulty in remembering facts, lower grades and/or a lowered level of self-confidence regarding school assignments;
- **behavioral** — disruptive classroom behavior, poor attendance, more frequent visits to the school nurse, increased absence due to "illness" or injury, greater frequency of accidents, withdrawal from school sports or other school activities, and/or acting-out, punishment-seeking or even violent behavior;
- **emotional** — greater need for teacher attention and support, apathy, a general loss of interest in school, altered relationships with staff and peers, greater feelings of anger or guilt, and sadness — an inability to enjoy life, including school. (Stevenson, 1986).

A school or classroom can be turned upside down by the physical and emotional demands of the grief process and the disruption which even a few of the possible reactions listed above can cause. The larger the number of affected students, the greater the disruption of the educational process. Some students are coping with the greater burden imposed by more than one loss. Multiple losses are so common that they should be seen as the rule and not an exception. Multiple losses can involve personal losses of each individual, or they may be of the type which affect an entire community.

In interviews with death education students, the two benefits most frequently identified were: a lessening of fear and anxiety regarding death, and improved communication by students. Young people said that before taking a death education course, they believed they could not discuss the topic of death. This silence increased their fear of death and hindered communication with those, such as family members, who might have offered support. After taking a death education course, students spoke of bringing class materials home and of discussing death and grief with family members, often for the first time. As students spoke more openly of the topic, they felt that their fear and anxiety lessened. As one student said, "Before I took a death education course I thought about death all the time, but I couldn't talk about it. Since taking this course I talk about death with a lot of people...so I don't have to think about it any more." (Stevenson, 1984) The object here is *not* to eliminate a fear of death, but to bring it to a level which is less threatening to a student. It is often said that "Knowledge is power" and in this case the knowledge provided is about dying, death, and grief. It is of greatest benefit to those students who have been forced to confront death in a personal way. However, because of individual differences such courses should be elective rather than required. The student must be willing to deal with this issue voluntarily.

Staff development programs and workshops have provided an ongoing means of staff preparation to assist bereaved students. Such professional development programs can also assist school personnel in helping students facing life-threatening illness.

Students Facing Life-Threatening Illness

Students who face life-threatening illness have special needs which differ from the bereaved child. The course of a life-threatening illness can force a young person to accept many losses and to anticipate others. However, the fact that death is a *possibility* is far different from the *reality* of a death that has already happened.

Recommendation #6 — Students facing life-threatening illness can be helped by teachers and classmates to feel connected to the class, to feel that they are not "different."

Students who face a life-threatening illness, such as cancer, leukemia, juvenile diabetes or AIDS say again and again that they "don't want to be different." The school plays a special role in making this possible. The student's work can be displayed in the classroom. The class can maintain contact with the student through letters and phone calls and can send work to be displayed by the absent student at home or in a hospital room.

As with bereaved children, regular communication is most helpful to all of the people involved—the ill student, the student's peers, the teacher and parents. The more aware the other students are of what is happening, the less likely they are to feel threatened by the recurring absence/presence of the sick child. The school nurse should also be brought into the classroom communication so that students with personal questions that they do not wish to bring up in class will have someone to whom they can turn for answers.

Recommendation #7 — The school can help students facing life-threatening illness, and their peers, to maintain hope.

The discussion of future goals can present a problem for some teachers. However, if the student is continuing to work on his/her studies and wants to go to college, such a goal should be encouraged. The presence of such a goal allows the student to focus on something outside of his/her illness. It can help the student to maintain hope.

Speaking as a teacher who has been in this situation, I am aware that having a student fighting a life-threatening illness is something which places a strain on classmates and on school staff. However, the school community can be a place of support and hope. It is often the first place to which young people wish to return when they enter remission or are discharged from the hospital.

There are excellent resources available for teachers in this position from the American Cancer Society.

Conclusions

Students cannot be shielded from the reality of death in their lives. School can play a positive role in preparing adolescents to cope with the reality of dying, death and grief and in helping younger children to deal with the grief they experience after the death of a relative or friend. To prepare for this role there are several recommended steps which schools should take:

1. Parents and teachers must establish and maintain ties so that each can inform the other about important developments in a child's life as they occur.
2. There is some information about death which is essential for all young people to know, regardless of cultural difference or religious beliefs.
3. If there are students in every school who must learn to cope

with the death of a relative or friend, schools should have protocols in place to use when such events occur.

4. Teachers need to be aware of specific actions they can take to aid
   bereaved students.
5. Death education programs should be in place as part of a preventive approach to grief-related problems in older students.
6. Students facing life-threatening illness can be helped by teachers and classmates to feel connected to the class, to feel that they
   are not "different."
7. The school can help students facing life-threatening illness, and
   their peers, to maintain hope.

Unique programs in our schools for students with special needs have
made great strides in helping these students to move past their special needs and to be able to cope with whatever they may face in the
future. Educators and parents must work together to create in our
schools a place where bereaved students and those facing life-threatening illness can find support for their special needs as well.

References and Recommended Readings

American Cancer Society, *When You Have A Student With Cancer*
(1980).

Cohn, J. *I Had A Friend Named Peter* (New York: William Morrow,
1987).

Critelli, C. "Parent Death In Childhood" Paper presented at the
Columbia-Presbyterian Medical Center Symposium *The Child and
Death*, New York City, New York (January 26, 1979).

Grollman, E.A. *Talking About Deaths A Dialogue Between Parent and
Child* (Boston: Beacon Press, 1990).

LaTour, K. *For Those Who Live: Helping Children Cope With the Death of
a Brother or Sister* (Omaha, Nebraska: Centering Corporation, 1983).

Metzgar, M.M. *Crisis In Schools; Is Your School Prepared?* (Seattle,
Washington: Margaret M. Metzgar, 1988).

O'Toole, D. *Growing Through Grief* (Burnsville, North Carolina: Mountain Rainbow Publications, 1989).

Stevenson, R.G. "A Death Education Course for Secondary Schools: 'Curing' Death Ignorance" Doctoral Dissertation (Fairleigh Dickinson University, Teaneck, NJ; 1984).

"Measuring the Effects of Death Education in the Classroom," in *Children and Death*, G.H. Paterson, Ed. (London, Ontario: King's College, 1986).

What Will We Do? Preparing A School Community to Cope With Crises (Amityville, NY: Baywood Press, 1994).

Section Four
Innovative Research

Throughout this book, we have sought to include chapters that review the state of what is known and thought about children, life-threatening illness and death. There has been a concern that the author or each chapter provide an overview that is written in style that is concise and free of an overemphasis on research that might limit its accessibility to the broad viewership of this teleconference.

Yet, research is the lifeblood of a field. It allows its theories, ideas and programs to be evaluated and refined. It brings whole new areas and concepts into focus.

In editing this book, it seemed important to introduce readers to the interesting research that is currently being done and that underlies the chapters of this book and the focus of the teleconference. Of the existing material, three articles seemed particularly worthwhile to present to our readers.

Many viewers and readers have already been exposed to the work of Myra Bluebond-Langner whose book *The Private Worlds of Dying Children* (Princeton, NJ: Princeton University Press, 1978) remains a classic in the field. In that work, Bluebond-Langner suggests that children with a terminal illness gradually understand the implications of their disease.

But Bluebond-Langner has not only explored the worlds of dying children but also of their well siblings. In this piece, she points out that many of these children live in houses of chronic sorrow. Their own lives are often contingent on their sibling's illness. And, Bluebond-Langner, reminds they often have to cope with their own confusing emotions while their parents' focus may be engaged elsewhere. Bluebond-Langner's article outlines a distinction so important in Anderson's chapter. A disease may infect a certain number of people, but so many others are affected by it. And Bluebond-Langner sensitizes caregivers to the critical needs of these affected siblings.

Two other articles are included because they expand our thoughts about the nature of grief. McClowry and her associates challenge perspectives that grief is timebound and resolved in a similar way for each affected family. McClowry in her research found that parents who faced the death of a child lived with that sense of loss for long periods of time. While some felt they "got over it," others described a more complex pattern where they found ways to fill this perpetual "empty space" or maintain a significant and therapeutic connection to the deceased child. It is not only adults that do that. Silverman, Nickman, and Worden, in their study of childhood bereavement also document the many ways that children continued a healthy sense of connection to their deceased parents.

Naturally, this chapter is limited both by space and the editor's own perception of significant researchers. Readers may wish to review the state of research themselves.

The bibliographies in the chapters should offer some direction. In addition, two journals, *Omega* and *Death and Dying Studies* are devoted exclusively to research on dying and death.

Worlds of Dying Children and their Well Siblings

10

Myra Bluebond-Langner

This paper examines the place of illness and death in the lives of healthy children and their ill siblings at the end stages of life. The behaviors that the children exhibit provide important insights into the children's views of their lives as well as their views of death.

Introduction

A child is dying of kidney disease, of cystic fibrosis, of cancer. We refer to the child as a "victim of chronic or terminal illness." But that child, that dying child, is not necessarily the only victim of chronic or terminal illness. The victims of chronic and terminal illness are not limited to the diagnosed patient. The destructive effects of such diseases spread to the families of those afflicted. New events and activities become part of the everyday lives of these families: time consuming care of the patient, trips to the hospital, the absence of family members during hospitalizations. A constant concern for the ill patient settles in for the duration. New feelings develop as well. Who would not occasionally resent the way in which one's life has been complicated by capricious chance? Yet what right do the healthy members have to feel such feelings, to think such thoughts? They do not look forward to permanent disability or to death. So begins for the family, for each and every member of that family, a cycle of feelings that includes anxiety, guilt, neglect, denial, anger, and depression.

I want to call your attention to some of the other "victims"—the well siblings of terminally ill children dying of cancer and cystic fibrosis. I want to explore with you the place that illness and death have in their worlds. But before doing that, I think it is important to

[This is the text of the 1988 Arthur G. Peterson Lecture, presented at the University of Florida, Gainesville, March 8, 1988.]

115

acquaint you with the world of the terminally ill child. For it is through observation and interaction with the dying child that the well sibling comes to know of disease and death. I will limit my remarks to the terminal phases of the illness. I will not discuss the behaviors one sees in earlier phases of the illness (e.g., diagnostic, relapses, exacerbations). The behaviors one sees before the child is terminal are very different from what one sees during the terminal phases. Later I will discuss some of those differences. For now, let us turn to the world of the terminally ill child.

Terminally Ill Children

While all terminally ill children become aware of the fact that they are dying before death is imminent, the acquisition and assimilation of information is a prolonged process. It is a process that involves not only learning about the disease, but also experiences in that disease world and changes in self-concept. In situations where the children are told their diagnosis and prognosis, I refer to the process as one of internalization. In situations where the children are not told, I refer to the process as one of discovery. The process, however, remains the same in both situations and is outlined in Figure 1.

In the first stage in the acquisition of information, the children learn that they have a serious illness. In the second stage, they learn the name of the drugs and their side effects. In the third stage they become aware of the purposes of various treatments and procedures. In the fourth stage, they are able to take all of these isolated bits and pieces of information and put them into a larger perspective, the cycle of relapses and remissions. At this point, however, the children do not incorporate death into the cycle. It is only when they reach the fifth stage that the children come to see the disease as having a terminal prognosis.

At the same time that the children pass through these stages in the acquisition of information, their view of themselves also changes. They move from a view of themselves as seriously ill to a view of themselves as ill and going to get better, to a view of themselves as always ill and going to get better, to a view of themselves as always ill and never going to get better, and finally, to a view of themselves as dying.

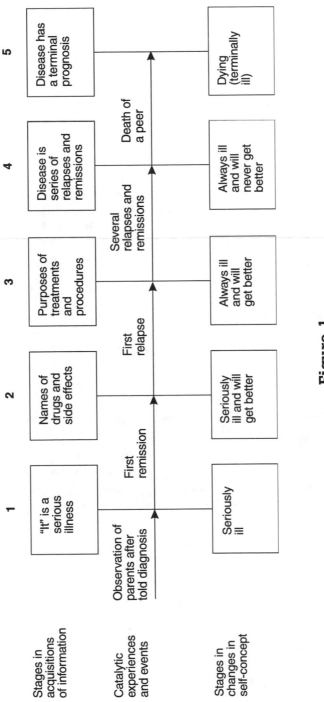

Figure 1

For children to pass through these stages though, certain significant experiences have to take place. The first stage follows upon observation of their parents and the reactions of others to the news of the diagnosis. The second stage comes with the first remission; the third with the first relapse; the fourth, after a series of relapses and remissions; and the fifth, on the death of a peer.

As you consider this process, it is important to bear in mind that information is cumulative, such that if a child is at stage 2 and another child dies, he or she will not necessarily see the disease or himself or herself as having a terminal prognosis. Also, experience in the disease world is the most critical factor in the child's coming to understand the disease. As you may have noticed, I have not mentioned age in this process. The children that we are going to be talking about are children between the ages of 5 and 12, all of whom became aware of the fact that they were dying before death was imminent. While their awareness of death did not vary by age, the way that they expressed it sometimes did.

If I had time, what I would like to do at this point is to detail each of the stages for you. But given the constraints of time, I'm going to jump to stage 4. At this point, the child, like the parents, comes to see the disease as something from which he or she will probably not recover. While the world is becoming increasingly closed to these children, they are still very much concerned about maintaining contact. The child is keenly aware of people's exits and entrances. And perhaps that is why the death of a peer can have the impact that it does. It is as if in a matter of sentences the child assimilates a great deal of information and comes to the conclusion that he or she is dying. For example, a nurse had come into Tom's room while he was sleeping to check his IV. On hearing her by his bed, Tom spoke.

> Tom: Jennifer died last night. I have the same thing, don't I?
> Nurse: But they are going to give you different medicines.
> Tom: What happens when they run out?
> Nurse: Well, maybe they will find more before then.

This kind of conversation, of which I will give several examples, I refer to as a disclosure of awareness conversation. The conversation follows the same format regardless of what the other person in the interaction might say. The child begins by mentioning someone who has died or is in danger of dying. He or she then attempts to establish the cause of death either through a statement or a hypothesis. Finally, the child compares himself or herself to the deceased. For example:

> Scott: You know Lisa?
> Myra: [Nods.]
> Scott: The one I played ball with. [Pause.] How did she die?
> Myra: She was sick, sicker than you are now.
> Scott: I know that. What happened?
> Myra: Her heart stopped beating.
> Scott [Hugging and crying]: I hope that never happens to me, but...

If the children recently discovered their prognosis, they talked about how different their condition was from that of the deceased, as in this conversation between a child I will call Benjamin and myself.

> Benjamin: Dr. Richards told me to ask you what happened to Sylvia. [Dr. Richards had said no such thing.]
> Myra: What do you think happened to Sylvia?
> Benjamin: Well, she didn't go to another hospital. Home?
> Myra: No. She was sick, sicker than you are now, and she died.
> Benjamin: She had nosebleeds. I had nosebleeds, but mine stopped.

Benjamin repeated this conversation with everyone he saw that day.

A more abstract version of a disclosure conversation occurred between a child I will call Stuart and myself after Stuart had been visited by a woman whose child had died 6 months earlier.

> Stuart: Do you drive to the hospital?
> Myra: No, I walk.
> Stuart: Do you walk at night?
> Myra [Noting the look on his face]: You wouldn't?
> Stuart: No, you would get shot. [Silence.] An ambulance would come and take you to the funeral home. And they would drain the blood out of you and wait 3 days and bury you.
> Myra: That's what happens when you die?
> Stuart: I saw them do it to my grandmother.
> Myra: I thought you told me you were here [in the hospital] when your grandmother died? [He was.]
> Stuart [Quickly]: It was my grandmother. They wait 3 days to

see if you're alive. I mean, they draw the blood after they wait 3 days. [Note: the child had been in the hospital 3 days. They had drawn blood, done a bone marrow, and told the parents that things were not good, but that they would try one more experimental drug.] That's what happens when you die. I'm going to get a new medicine put in me tonight.

If the child had known the prognosis for some time, he or she would talk about how much he or she was like the deceased, as in this conversation between a child I will call Mary, her mother, and an occupational therapy student when they were packing to go home.

OTS: What should I do with these, Mary? [Holding up the papers dolls that Mary, on an earlier occasion, said looked the way she did before she became ill.]

Mary [Who hadn't said anything the entire time that they were packing to go home]: Put them in their grave in the Kleenex box.

Mother: Well, that's the first thing you offered to do since the doctors said that we could go home.

Mary: I'm burying them. [Carefully arranges them between sheets of Kleenex.]

There were many children who did not engage in such full-blown disclosure of awareness conversations, but they made their awareness known in other ways. One way was through simple declarative statements like "I'm not going to be here for your birthday," "I'm never going back to school again," or "They're not buying me a coat to grow into this winter." Interestingly, these statements accomplish the same things as the longer conversation. To say, for example, "I'm not getting a coat to grow into," or "I'm never going back to school," is to say, "I'm not like other children. When you are dead or you die, you don't go to school, and people don't buy you coats to grow into."

These statements are a telegraphic form of the disclosure of awareness conversations. There is a mention of death, but it is one's own. The death is implied rather than stated. The comparison this time is not to other deceased children, but rather to one's self, to the world of healthy children.

In the examples I have given, you may have noticed a lack of references to heaven. Very few of the children mentioned heaven when they spoke to me. That does not mean that heaven was not a part of their world. It just was not part of the world as they communicated it to me. I guess I don't bring out the heaven in people. Perhaps that is the clergy's job. But whatever it was, heaven did not come through in their discussions with me. This raises some important methodological issues. For example, while the responses we receive from children reflect their views of death, they also reflect their views of the interviewer. When I spoke with the children they tended not to take death further than the grave. Grave imagery was far more prevalent than heaven imagery. Their view of death was expressed in terms of what they would miss here on earth.

It is also important to note the context in which the disclosure of awareness conversations arose. The conversations always seemed to come up when one least expected them, when one was least prepared—passing by a child's room on the way to do something else, for example.

A quality of "out of nowhere" was characteristic of many of the statements the children made with regard to death—not only their more direct serious statements, but also those tinged with gallows humor. For example, one child on waking from a nap said, "Fooled you, I'm not dead yet." Another child, when asked if he could be made more comfortable because he had IVs going in both arms, said, "No, I'm practicing for my coffin."

In general, death and disease imagery increased as other topics decreased. The children spoke far less about the efficacy of various drugs in the end stages of life than they did in the early part of the disease when remissions were achieved. Notably absent from these children's conversations was any long-range future orientation. They did not talk about what they were going to be when they grew up, and they became angry when other people did. The furthest into the future that they would seem to go was the next holiday or event.

While the children's long-range future orientation diminished, they were still very much concerned about the amount of time that they had left. Staff often remarked on the activity and urgency that so often followed the death of a patient. Some children verbalized it on those days with statements like, "Don't waste time," or "I can't waste time." These children were having their time cut short and they knew it.

There was also a general lack of interest in typical childhood paraphernalia. Often what interest there was (when they were not too debilitated to pay attention) was filled with death and disease imagery. As one play therapist remarked, "Give 'em crayon, draws graves." One of the most popular books was *Charlotte's Web*, especially the chapter where Charlotte dies. Children buried toys in graves and often refused to play with toys from other diseased children. Among many of the children it was as if a taboo had developed around the names of diseased children and their belongings.

Perhaps what was most remarkable in all of these children was an overall shift in behavior from strategies that we would view as engaging people to strategies that we would view as disengaging people. There were frequent displays of anger, banal chit-chat, withdrawal. Children and adults said that these kinds of behaviors came about when things became unbearable. They provided individuals with an excuse for leaving and thereby a way of returning.

Myra: Jeffrey, why do you always yell at your mother?
Jeffrey: Then she won't miss me when I'm gone.
Myra [To Jeffrey's mother]: Why does Jeffrey always yell at you?
Mother: Look, Myra, he knows when I can't take it anymore in that room, and he knows that if he yells, I'll leave. He also knows I'll come back.

It was as if these disengaging or distancing behaviors were almost a kind of rehearsal for the final separation. As the people at St. Christopher's Hospice in London say, "Withdrawal is not necessarily a hostile act."

The behaviors that children display in the fifth stage reflect a variety of views of death. Imbedded in each of the aforementioned actions and statements are views of death as separation, mutilation, loss of identity, the result of a biological processes that is inevitable and irreversible. Death comes across as many things, even contradictory things at once. For example, one 5-year-old concerned about separation who talked about worms eating him and refused to play with toys from deceased children was the same 5-year-old who knew that the drugs had run out and demanded that time not be wasted. So too, the 9-year-old girl who drew pictures of herself on blood red crosses knew that it was the medication that was making her liver bad. She was the same 9-year-old who could not bear to have her mother leave her for a moment and carefully avoided the names of the deceased children and their belongings.

I mention and underscore these seeming contradictions because they raise important questions about the development of children's views of death. In each of these cases, we find views of death that one would expect for children their age as well as ones we would not. I regret that time does not permit me to develop this point. So let me just give you an idea to reflect on later. When a child is dying, his or her experiences are very different from other children of the same age, and hence the accepted developmental model of children's view of death is not as applicable for the dying child as it would be for healthy children. Let us turn now from the world of the dying child to the world of the well sibling.

Well Siblings

The well siblings of terminally ill children live in houses of chronic sorrow. The signs of sorrow, illness, and death are everywhere, whether or not they are spoken of. The signs are written on parent's faces: "My mother always looks tired now," and "Even my dad's crying a lot." The signs are there in hushed conversations: "You learn everything by listening in on the [phone] extension." The signs of illness and death are there in the time the parents do not have to share with the well sibling: "My mom used to come watch me play ball; she doesn't anymore. The sorrow comes through in outbursts of anger, short tempers and irritability: "My parents fight all the time now, one minute she's [child's] mother all lovey-dovey and the next minute, whammo, do this, do that." Illness makes for interrupted schedules. As one child said, "Who can plan?" Plans must often be changed. On hearing that the family wouldn't be going on a camping trip as planned, the younger brother of a terminally ill child said, "So what else is new?" And sometimes life-styles are changed. Many researchers have reported the financial strain that chronic illness places on a family budget. Some have listed financial strain among the top three sources of stress. For the well siblings, there is often less contact with peers: "I can't have my friends over because they may have a cold and give it to my brother." Finally, the signs of illness, of death and sorrow are there on their ill brother's or sister's face: "He can't do much now on account of his low platelets," "She just lies there now with the oxygen in her nose," and "Why is it she even looks dead now?" These children are living in a situation quite unlike their peers', quite unlike the situation that most adults find themselves in.

What happens to the well siblings in this situation? Many experience a change in their role in the family, a change in status. During hospitalization, the well siblings often are shifted from place to place, from a relative's house to a neighbor's house, to home again for an evening. Some well siblings see themselves as the less favored child in the family. Often the well sibling parents the parent: "I must take care of Mommy now." In some families, the well sibling is the caretaker of the ill sibling, baby-sitting or helping with the therapy or equipment. Some become what Goffman (l) calls "non- persons." They are there, but they are not there. They overhear conversations, but are not part of them. The well sibling may accompany the child to the clinic or to the hospital, but is not present during the examinations.

When a brother or sister is dying, the well siblings often find themselves not getting what one usually expects from one's parents, what they themselves once received from their parents. The well siblings experience difficulty receiving the kind of care, attention, support and nurturing that they once knew: "Nobody has time for me right now. I must always wait." But when a sibling is dying, a parent's attention is elsewhere. The well children often feel alone, unsupported, neglected, or the flip side, overprotected. As one boy said to me, "I can't turn around without her on me. Where are you going? What are you doing? When will you be back? Who is going with you?"

Well siblings often feel confused. They are confused about the information that they are receiving about their sibling's status. They receive information from a variety of sources—the ill brother or sister, the parent, their own observations. Some of the information is correct, some incorrect. Often the information is incomplete. The well sibling's knowledge of the disease may be limited to what he or she was told when the ill sibling was diagnosed, a time when the child was young and, hence, told very little. Because of the parents' reluctance to speak about the ill child's condition as the disease progressed, the well sibling's information might not have been updated.

Well siblings also feel confused about the shifts in their parents' emotions. Some well siblings feel confused about who they are and who they are supposed to be. Sometimes they feel like they should be sometimes like the dying child, sometimes like a parent, and sometimes, as one boy said, "just blend into the woodwork."

It is not unusual to hear well siblings express feelings of betrayal, that their parents were not honest with them: "I wish they'd tell me the truth. I can take it."

It is important to point out, however, that not all children feel betrayed. Many of the children said that they did not want to know, at least not from their parents, how really ill their brother or sister was. They feel it would be too hard to hear it from their parents.

Well siblings often feel rejected. Several saw their parent's preoccupation with the ill sibling as a rejection of them: "Nobody cares about me and my needs anymore," or

> The gifts don't make up for the hurts and other things inside of me. It doesn't make anything, you know. You may smile on the outside, but on the inside, it hurts. It doesn't take care of the pain or anything.

The feelings and the experiences that I have just described exist not because parents do not want to do what is right for their well children, but because often they can't. The demands, physically, emotionally, not to mention financially, of caring for a terminally ill child—be it at home or in the hospital—are great. The demands are most keenly felt around the area of attention, which to children is the hallmark of love. Parents spoke of wanting to give the well siblings more attention, but not being able to. Well siblings spoke of wanting more attention, of not getting enough, but also knowing why they could not have more attention. The well siblings and the parents are in a bind: "It's tough when she gets extra attention, but she has to get extra attention so that she'll live," "My mother tries to make up for the attention she gives him, but she can't make up for it all," or "Dad treats him better because he doesn't have much of a life. He's going to die. But what about me? You know, I could get hit by a car or something."

It's important to bear in mind for the well siblings of children suffering from chronic and terminal illness the feelings of betrayal, of anger, of rejection, and of lack of attention were not necessarily there throughout the course of the illness. My recent research with families of children with cystic fibrosis (2, 3) shows that for long periods of time, these families appear very much like other families. They are not homes of chronic sorrow. The feelings that are there in the terminal stages are not necessarily there in the earlier stages of the disease.

And when they are, they are either muted or expressed quite directly. For example, I recall walking into the clinic waiting room and seeing the two well brothers of a CF patient, who was doing rather well, telling their mother that they were hungry and asking her if she would either take them to get something to eat or let them go on their own. The mother asked them to wait until Zoe, their sister, had been examined. The brothers replied, almost in chorus, "If Zoe wanted something to eat, you'd go get it for her right away."

In the final stages of the disease, though, the siblings feel less justified in making some of these same demands. For example, when one mother asked her son, "You feel like you want more, most of the attention?" he responded, "No, I don't want most of the attention. I know Ellen has CF, and she needs most of the attention." Nonetheless, he demonstrated his desire for attention in other ways. Like many well brothers of cystic fibrosis patients, he put on a great deal of weight and he was behind in his school work.

That the majority of parents are able to give their children, well and ill, so much of what they needed for so long, up until the terminal period, is due in large measure to the strategies that these families adopt to contain the intrusion that such a disease makes into their lives. While time does not permit a discussion of these strategies, suffice it to say, that these were strategies for dealing with a chronic illness and they were no longer used, no longer could be used, once the child's condition became terminal.

Returning to the terminal period, but shifting from the well sibling's relation to the parents to the well sibling's relationship with the ill brother or sister, we notice that the well brother also has difficulty getting what he once did from his ill brother or sister. Throughout the course of the illness, siblings struggle to maintain themselves in a relationship of give and take. As the disease progresses, as the child's physical condition deteriorates and hospitalizations become more frequent, elements of the sibling relationship (companionship, mutual aid, support, self-definition, communication) become problematic. During hospitalization, the well sibling is often left without a companion. Contact is neither regular nor in a familiar context. Mutual aid declines. Siblings often find that they cannot give reciprocally to one another. Ill siblings often refuse gestures of help from their well siblings. For example, while Jake lay dying, complaining of his back hurting him and not being able to breathe, his brothers offered to rub his back. He pushed them away saying, "No, no, not you. Only Mommy now." The ill child's alliances shift from a closeness to both the parent and the sibling to a closeness with the parent divorced from that of the sibling.

Using the sibling as a means of self-definition also becomes problematic. One's sibling is like a mirror image, but what a distorted image stares back. Feelings of protection and worry replace those of identification.

> Lenny: I think about her all the time.
> Myra: Even in school?
> Lenny: [Nods.]
> Myra: What do you do in school?
> Lenny: I just think about her.

Communication is often distorted as particular subjects are avoided: "We talk about everything except the CF," or "I don't want to talk about her CF because it might upset her."

Ironically, however, if once the siblings know the prognosis they do not begin to talk to each other, a distance is created in the relationship that can last until the patient's death: "We [my ill brother and I] weren't that close. We didn't talk. But my sister, she talked to him a lot. That made them very close." Now add to all the well sibling's feelings the normal feelings of jealousy, rivalry, hostility that are there in any sibling relationship, feelings that have been heightened by the disease, and add for good measure the feelings of guilt that come from seeing and acknowledging that one's peer— one's brother or sister—is dying, and the behaviors seen in well siblings become far more understandable. The well sibling is struggling with thoughts and fears that are not so easily managed, and often he or she struggles alone. The conflicting thoughts and feelings are well expressed in the following interchange among a therapist, a well child named Karen, whose sister, Linda, has cystic fibrosis and whose brother, Chip, died of cystic fibrosis, and their mother.

> Karen [Who is at this point in the discussion, crying]: I remember I used to like running around, and Chip would say, you know, "You quit running," and complain about what I was doing and stuff.
> Therapist: It was hard for you to do normal things because they would bother Chip, is that right? Did you feel like a bad person for doing that?"
> Karen: [Nods.]

Therapist: Do you still feel like maybe you hurt Chip? Does that still make you feel bad?

Karen: [Nods.]

Therapist: Have you ever said that before, Karen?

Karen: No. I worry about Linda because I don't want her to die. Because, you know, she's almost my best friend and she'll play with me.

Therapist: She's your best friend?

Karen: Uh-huh. And sometimes she won't play with me 'cause she doesn't feel good and I get sad and stuff, you know.

Mother: Karen, you know Chip had these bad, bad headaches because he wasn't getting the oxygen that he was supposed to be getting. And really your running around had nothing to do with his headaches. It was just his lungs were so bad.

Karen [Almost inaudibly]: I know that, but I still think it's my fault.

Ultimately then, these children must face the death of their brothers and sisters. Their first words, on hearing of that death, often provide us with important clues as to what these children are thinking and feeling. In some cases, they may be the only clue that we get for a long time. It is not unusual to hear something like, "Good, now I can have all of his toys." Or in the words of another child, "I wanted my own room anyway."

If we step back for a moment and unpack those statements, I think we will hear some other things in their somewhat shocking remarks. We hear anger, "You left me." We also hear jealousy, "You had more than I did." And like so many adults arguing over the deceased's possessions, we also hear a desire to hold onto something. There are also the sounds of pain and loss. As one child who no longer played with the toys that he eagerly took at his brother's death put it, "I don't want them [toys] without John here. It's no fun." There are heightened feelings of loneliness. Siblings will often talk about how quiet the house has become since their brother or sister died.

Running through their statements is a great deal of ambivalence, ambivalence that was there throughout the entire relationship and throughout the entire illness. These ambivalent feelings are coupled with feelings of guilt. As one brother put it, "I'm glad it was him and not me. I know that's not nice, but I can't help it." Or in the words of another, "Do you think I'm cold-blooded? I couldn't stand him that way, just lying there with oxygen in his nose yelling, 'Rub me, rub me.'" Some siblings feel responsible: "I gave her that pneumonia."

It is important to bear in mind that many of the children felt that they could not express their feelings to their parents, that their parents were already too upset, and they did not want to upset them anymore. This is not to say that the well siblings' feelings do not come out in other ways.

John Gilenski, psychologist and priest at Oakland Children's Hospital, has found that the two most common ways the children exhibit their feelings are through sleep disorders and acting out (personal communication). He also has found that many children also engage in little adult behaviors. Other behaviors that have been reported for well siblings include: acting like the deceased, experiencing psychosomatic illnesses, fearing illness, fearing losing control, regressing, being unable to separate, refusing to mention the deceased, losing appetite or overeating, bed-wetting, and feeling depressed. I mention these behaviors not because they are going to happen (the frequency and prevalence of these phenomena are not known), but because they are things that serve to put us on warning, things that we should be looking at, that we may want to watch for in bereaved siblings.

In conclusion, how can we help the dying child and his or her siblings? What can we do? I think the most important thing we can do is to take our cues from the child, to tell the child what he or she wants to know, on his or her terms. The issue is not whether to tell, but rather when to tell, why you are telling, and who should do the telling.

I am reminded of that famous sex education story, which you probably know. After a hard day at school, Johnny sits down at the kitchen table to enjoy a glass of milk with his mom. Munching on a cookie, Johnny asks, "Where did I come from?" Mom opens her eyes real wide, takes a good strong, stiff drink of milk, and begins a lecture on the facts of life. Johnny eats a few more cookies, swallows the last of his milk, and comments, "Oh. Stevie said he came from New York."

The child has different needs, different concerns, at different times. The challenge before us is to recognize these different needs, these different concerns, at the time he brings them to us.

References

1. Goffman, E. (1959). *The presentation of self in everyday life.* Garden City, New York: Anchor, Doubleday.
2. Bluebond-Langner, M. (1978). *The private worlds of dying children.* Princeton: Princeton University.
3. Bluebond-Langner, M. (1985). Living with cystic fibrosis: A family affair. In D. Schidlow (Ed.), *Cystic fibrosis: Soma and psyche.* New Jersey: McNeil Laboratories.

Detachment Revisited: The Child's Reconstruction of a Dead Parent

11

Phyllis R. Silverman, Steven Nickman,
J. William Worden

During the year following a parent's death, children in a community-based sample were found to have developed an inner construction of the dead parent. This continued, though altered, relationship appeared to facilitate their coping with the loss and with accompanying changes in their lives. Implications for understanding the bereavement process and for interventions focusing on detachment are discussed.

The observation that children maintain a connection to deceased parents is not new (Bolby, 1980; Dietrich & Shabad, 1989; Jacobs, Koston, Dasl, & Ostfeld, 1987; Klass, 1988; Miller, 1971; Moss & Moss, 1981; Osterweis, Solomon, & Greene, 1984; Rubin, 1985; P.R. Silverman, 1986; Silverman & Silverman, 1979; Worden, 1991). However, there are different interpretations of this observation and different theories about the nature of the connection. In their studies of parents whose children had died, Klass (1988) and Rubin (1985) concluded that remaining connected to the deceased seems to be a necessary part of the bereavement process—that it is adaptive and facilitates an accommodation to the death. Lifton (1979) described strategies that mourners used to provide the deceased with "symbolic immortality." Others (Furman, 1984; Volkan, 1981) have reported that for successful mourning to take place, the mourner must disengage from the deceased, that is, let go of the past. This experi-

A revised version of a paper submitted to the Journal in August 1991. Research was funded by grant MH41791 from the National Institute of Mental Health, and by grants from the National Funeral Directors Association and from the Hillenbrand Corporation. Authors are at the Department of Psychiatry, Massachusetts General Hospital, Boston.

ence of the deceased is often thought of as symptomatic of psychological problems (Dietrich & Shabad, 1989; Miller, 1971). In her study of bereaved preschool children attending a therapeutic nursery school, Furman (1974) noted that it is important for children to loosen their ties to their deceased parents and suggested that therapists should encourage detachment behavior. This formulation has its roots in Freud's (1917/1957) observations that patients best resolved their grief when they gradually withdrew the mental energy they had extended toward the lost love object and reinvested this energy in new relationships.

The conceptualizations that prescribe detachment were drawn primarily from clinical interactions with troubled people. Thus, they may be based on a sample that is overly representative of individuals who had recourse to relatively primitive defense mechanisms, such as denial. These people, who may have experienced greater than normal difficulty in accepting the reality of the death, were more likely to exhibit an inappropriate investment in the past (Furman, 1974; Volkan, 1981). The present paper, based on interviews with children who had lost a parent, is an attempt to broaden our understanding of the bereavement process and the ways in which the deceased is experienced by a nonclinical population.

In the psychoanalytic literature on children, efforts to maintain a connection to the deceased parent are seen as internal representations of the dead parent (Dietrich & Shabad, 1989; Jacobson, 1965; Rochlin, 1959, 1965; Schafer, 1968; Wolfenstein, 1973). Identification and internalization are considered processes that the bereaved use to keep an aspect of the deceased with them forever (Furman, 1984; Volkan, 1981). These inner representations are described as unchanging. Dietrich and Shabad (1989) emphasized the paradoxical character of the inner representation of the deceased: one that is both frozen in time and timeless—immortalized and lost simultaneously. Schafer (1968) regarded a bereaved child's inner representations of the lost parent as persisting unmodified and inaccessible to secondary-process thinking.

The concept of internalization, however, does not fully describe the process that bereaved children undergo. What the authors observed was more colorful, dynamic, and interactive than the term internalization suggests. In fact, this inner representation was not buried in the unconscious or stable over time. The child was aware of the inner representation, and the representation seemed to change with time as the child developed. Playwright Robert Anderson (1974) used the word relationship to describe his experience of the deceased, as did such researchers as Klass (1988) and Rubin (1985).

Rizzuto (1979) observed that the process of constructing inner representations involves the whole individual and that these representations are not static, but grow and change with the individual's development and maturation. She also noted the importance of the role of others in the construction of inner representations of significant people in her subjects' lives. Construction, she suggested, is partly a social activity. This observation is supported by the findings of Rosenblatt and Elde (1990), who studied bereaved families and found that grief work included maintaining connections with memories of the deceased. Mourners kept these memories "alive" by remembering, both in solitude and in the company of others, while integrating their memories into the present and into relationships with others.

A helpful family environment has positive facilitating effects. While individual family members have their "internalization," or inner representation of the deceased, the family as a whole may also have communal or shared representations, which may be experienced by individual members as existing or proceeding from outside the self; these can be altered as people and relationships change. Klass (1988) made a similar observation about the importance of others in helping bereaved parents maintain an active "relationship" with their dead children.

An analogous situation may occur with the disclosure of the fact of adoption to a child who was placed in infancy (Nickman, 1985). How well the adoptive parents are able to remain in touch with the child's developing internal representation of the birthparents can affect the child's self-esteem, personality development, and overall level of functioning. How well the adoptive parents help their child build a realistic representation of the birthparents that is compatible with the child's changing ability to understand is also a factor. With a child who is adopted later, the experience is similar to that of the bereaved child because the child is old enough to remember his or her birthparents.

The authors propose that it may be normative for mourners to maintain a presence and connection with the deceased and that this presence is not static. Just as the adopted child faces the question, "How could they give me up?" and deals with the birthparents' motivation over a period of years so the bereaved child must deal with how and why the parent died and what the parent's presence may have been like had it continued over time. One cannot deal with a loss without recognizing *what* is lost.

The construction of the lost parent is an ongoing cognitive process. The nature of the construction of the deceased is connected to the child's developmental level, with particular reference to children's changing ability to know themselves and to know others (Kegan, 1982; Piaget, 1954). For example, a critical developmental shift takes place when a child moves from seeing others in terms of how these others can meet his or her needs to seeing others as people with needs of their own and with whom some reciprocity is required for a relationship to be sustained. Although the deceased does not change, the child's ability to understand a given set of information about this person will change as the child matures.

The word *construction* derives from the Latin *struere*, to make something out of component parts; to construe is to analyze or set out logically the figurative aspects of a thing. In the psychological literature, constructivism refers to a theoretical position that regards persons or systems as constituting or constructing their own reality (Gergen, 1985). The authors see the child's attempt to maintain a connection to a dead parent as an active effort to make sense of the experience of loss and to make it part of the child's reality.

Data to be reported in this paper, drawn from a longitudinal study of the impact of a parent's death on school-age children, suggest a process of adaptation and change in the postdeath relationship and the construction and reconstruction of new connections. On the basis of these observations, the authors posit that learning to remember and finding a way to maintain a connection to the deceased that is consistent with the child's cognitive development and family dynamics are aspects of an accommodation process that allows the child to go on living in the face of the loss. The present paper investigates the elements from which this connection is made and describes what the connection looks like phenomenologically.

Child Bereavement Study

The Child Bereavement Study is a prospective study of children aged 6–17, one of whose parents has died. Families representing a range of socioeconomic and ethnic backgrounds were recruited from communities in the greater Boston area; 70% of the families were Catholic, reflecting the large concentration of Roman Catholics in this region. Interviews were conducted in the family home with each child and with the surviving parent at four months, one year, and then two years after the death (Silverman & Worden, 1992).

Seventy families with 125 children were interviewed. There were an almost equal number of boys and girls in the sample, with an average age of 11.6 years. Seventy-two percent of the children had lost a father and 28% a mother. The average age of the surviving parent was 41 years, with a range of 30 to 57 years for the surviving mothers and 33 to 50 years for the surviving fathers. In the case of 58% of the children (34 boys and 38 girls), the parent had died after a long illness.

For most couples (91%), this was their only marriage, and the mean length of their marriage had been 17 years. The modal number of children was two. In nine of the families, the child who participated in the study was an only child.

Family incomes after the death ranged from less than $10,000 a year to more than $50,000, with a median income range of $20,000–$29,000. Before the death, men were the primary breadwinners in the families. Many women worked part time outside the home, providing the family with a second income.

Data presented in this paper were taken primarily from the first two semistructured research interviews with these bereaved children and their surviving parents at four months and then at one year after the death. Where appropriate, data from the third interview were used. All the interviews were taped; if a tape was not transcribed, the authors listened to it. These interviews included questions regarding the parent's death, the child's mourning behavior, and the child's thoughts about the deceased in part informed by one of the author's prior research on bereaved children (Silverman, 1989; Silverman & Silverman,]979).

Additional qualitative data were drawn from the children's responses to the Child's Understanding of Death questionnaire (Smilansky, 1987). The analysis of data followed that recommended by Strauss (1987), leading to the development of a theory of the bereavement process that is grounded in the data (Glaser & Strauss,]967). The authors studied a sample of these interviews to identify themes and then read additional records to determine whether the same themes were present (Strauss, 1987). The remainder of this paper describes the elements from which a connection to the deceased is constructed.

Awareness of Death

The children's responses were initially examined to see if their efforts to connect with the deceased were the consequences of a faulty understanding of the concept of death. Findings from research on non-bereaved children raise questions about the age at which a child understands the irreversibility and finality of death (Lonetto, 1980). These bereaved children, regardless of their age, seemed aware of the meaning of death. One seven-year-old girl had no doubt about the finality of her father's death: "Sometimes I want to talk to him, but I go to sleep fast so I won't think about his being gone." A ten-year-old said: "He's not with me, and it hurts."

It was with great difficulty that these children accustomed themselves to the fact that their parents were dead. The contrast between presence and absence often seemed too difficult for them to contemplate, and their discomfort was apparent. In response to the standardized question, "What does it mean when someone dies?" a ten-year-old boy said, "I can't think about that." It seemed impossible to think that his father was gone. Some children, especially those whose parents died suddenly, talked about the shock they felt when they heard the news.

Their new reality required an understanding of death that is not typical of non-bereaved children of the same ages. A 12-year-old girl whose mother died after a long illness said that she could not talk about her mother because it "simply hurts too much." She added: "However, I don't want her to come back and be in such pain." When asked how he felt after his father's death, one 13-year-old boy said plaintively: "I don't know. . . . I just know he's not here anymore." The connection to the deceased cannot be dismissed as merely a way of denying the finality of the loss. The special tension in these children was clear. Although they were aware that their parents were dead, they experienced their parents as still existing in themselves and in their world. This duality caused cognitive dissonance for some and may have accounted for some of the inarticulateness seen shortly after the loss.

Strategies of Connection

Five categories were identified that reflect the child's efforts to maintain a connection to the deceased parent during this period: 1) making an effort to locate the deceased, 2) actually experiencing the deceased in some way, 3) reaching out to initiate a connection, 4) remembering, and 5) keeping something that belonged to the deceased. The majority of the children reported some activity in each area. There seemed to be no significant relationship between the type of death or the gender or age of the child and any of these responses. These aspects are discussed next, along with anecdotal data from interviews with the children.

Locating the Deceased

When asked where they thought the dead parent was presently, most of the children were able to locate the deceased. Of the 125 children, 92 (74%) believed in a place called "heaven" and that once dead, this was where their parents were; the other 33 (26%) were uncertain what they believed. There was no relationship between a child's age and his or her belief about an afterlife, nor was there any relationship between a child's belief system and how frequently the child dreamed or thought about the dead parent.

Although 70% of the sample were Roman Catholic and Catholic theology encourages these children to believe in the existence of heaven and in a life after death, there was no statistical relationship between the children's expressed beliefs and their religious background. Many non-Catholic children shared a similar belief system in which their parents had some form of existence in a place called "heaven." Even children in their early teens, who were otherwise developmentally and cognitively sophisticated, did not always distinguish between the state of being of the spirit and the body. Many continued to endow the deceased, now residing in heaven, with concrete attributes of a living person, e.g., that dead people see, hear, feel, and move. Others acknowledged a difference between the body that was buried and the soul that was in heaven, but they still endowed the soul with living qualities of vision, hearing, and mobility.

By contrast, matched nonbereaved control children were less likely to endow a deceased person with living attributes. Locating the deceased in a distant place (heaven) seemed to help the bereaved children make sense of their experience: although the deceased cannot see, feel, and move here, they may be able to do so in the place to which they have gone (a place that cannot be seen from here).

The words of a 14-year-old Catholic boy whose father died reflected this belief:

> I want my father to see me perform. If I said a dead person can't see, then I would not be able to have my wish that he see what I am doing. I believe that the dead see, hear, move. Don't ask me how, I just believe it. Heaven is a mysterious place. My father is with all the other relatives that died.

Belief in heaven allowed this boy to maintain a sense that his father was still in his life. A 17-year-old Jewish girl, two years after her father died, was clear about the permanency and finality of death, as could be expected, given her age. In her religious education the concept of heaven or an afterlife was not mentioned. However, in her response to a question about whether the dead can see or hear, she said:

> Yes, the dead can see and hear. It's what I would *like* to think, so he could hear comforting words and . . . that maybe he can see significant events in my life.

A similar cognitive construction was made by a 15-year-old girl who both saw her father in heaven and recognized that some of what she was experiencing was of her own making:

> I think heaven is not a definite place. . . . I know I'm not imagining him . . . it's not as if I actually see him standing there, but I feel him and, like, in my mind I hear his voice.

Experiencing the Deceased

Believing that their dead parents were watching them was an extension of this construction of the parents being in heaven and provided these children with yet another way of connecting with their dead parents. Of the 125 children, 101 (81%) felt that their deceased parents were watching them, and of those who felt watched, 71 (57%) were "scared" by this feeling. These children's uneasiness was related to their fear that their dead parent might not approve of what they were doing. As an 11-year-old boy said:

> I sometimes think he is watching me. It scares me because sometimes he might see me do something he wouldn't like. Like,

it's weird . . . it's not scary . . . like if you're doing something, like if someone's watching you, you don't do it, if it's bad. You don't do it if someone's watching.

This boy saw his father in the role of disciplinarian, and his feelings about his father included experiencing him as a helpful external control to supplement his incompletely formed superego. A teenage girl talked about how important good grades were for her mother. She said almost playfully that she could imagine her mother "yelling in heaven if I didn't do well in school."

In contrast, a child who did not have a good relationship with her father pictured him in a dream with a mean facial expression, but she could not make out his attitude toward her with any certainty. The dream frightened her and seemed to reflect an aspect of their relationship before his death that was not affirming of the child. It is apparent that, whether the parent was a disciplinarian, a nurturer, or one whose response might be unpredictable, the child experienced the parent in a way that reflected aspects of their relationship before the death.

Some children experienced their parents as communicating with them in a benevolent way that reflected the parents' status as spirits. One nine-year-old boy saw flashing colored dots in his bedroom at night and said he liked to think that it was his mother trying to be in touch with him. When he asked his father if it was possible, his father allowed the possibility and did not try to rationalize the experience away. An adolescent girl noticed a puff of wind blowing open the door of a restaurant where both she and her mother had worked and thought of it as her mother's presence coming to visit. This perception became a standing, good-natured joke between her and the others working in the restaurant.

Another way of experiencing the deceased was through dreams. Many children (56%, N= 69) dreamed about their parents and, for almost all of them (N=63), the parents were alive in the dreams. As one child put it:

I dreamed he met me on the way home from school and that he hugged me. Then I woke up. I felt so sad that I won't have that anymore.

Even though the children felt sad when faced with the fact that their parents' presence was only a dream, some children found these dreams comforting:

When I wake up from these dreams. I know she's gone, but when I dream. it feels like she is there and it's reality.

I am not sure but l hear his voice. It's probably in my dreams. He tells me he likes what I did, that I did real good.

Experiencing the deceased in this way tempered the pain and provided an occasion for the child to get parental approval: "It feels good to remember, to feel that he is still part of the family."

Children who found their deceased parents available to them in this way attributed some initiative to the parents and saw themselves as recipients. At some level, they knew that this construction was probably coming from something within themselves. This understanding may be similar to what Weisman (1972) called "middle knowledge": a partial awareness of the reality of death that forms the best compromise between an unpleasant truth and a wished-for state of events.

Reaching Out to the Deceased

Children also took some initiative to keep a connection. Visiting the cemetery was one way of actively seeking a place where they could "find" the deceased. For many, the cemetery was the place where they had the last contact with their parents. A 12-year-old girl whose mother had died said: "l go to the cemetery when I feel sad and I need someone to talk with." "Going to the cemetery makes me feel close." A 15-year-old boy, who passed the cemetery on his way home from school, stated:

I don't talk about it much, but I stop by to visit about once a week. I tell him about my day and things I've done.

Speaking to the deceased was another way of bringing the parent into the child's life. Seventy-one children (57%) spoke to their deceased parents. The initiative to choose the place was clearly with the child. A teenage girl said: "l say 'Hi, how are you?' when I go by her picture in the house." A 10-year-old boy reported: "In my mind, I talk to him; I tell him what I did today, about the fish I caught and that I did real good." Although 43% (N= 29) of these children, mostly younger, felt they received an answer, they were not usually able to tell us what their parents said. A 15-year-old girl remarked: "It's not that I heard him, but in my head l felt he said, 'You'll be OK. Carry on.'" A 16-year-old described her experience one year after her mother died:

> My mother was my friend. I could talk to her about anything. I talk to her, but she can't respond. She doesn't tell me what to do, but like she helps me—I can't explain it.

The ability to take an active role in relation to the death of their parents was reflected in the children's answers to the question, "What advice would you give another child who had lost a parent?" Some children could not answer this question and responded, "I don't know" or "I can't think of anything." These were the same children who did not dream about or talk to their deceased parents. They did not seem to have a place, as yet, for the deceased in their lives. The majority of children, however, did have suggestions, and most counseled fortitude. They said they would advise another child "not to let it get you down all the time" and that "it's possible to carry on." They also said, "It's best to think about the person who died and to remember the good times that you had." "Just think of them as often as you can. It helps to go to the cemetery a lot to let them know." These responses reflected the ability of some children to organize their experience and to reflect on what would be helpful to others in the same plight.

Waking Memories

The dead parents were present in the children's waking thoughts as well. These waking thoughts involved both reflection and memory. At the four-month interview, 90% of those responding were still thinking about their deceased parents at least several times a week. When asked what they thought about, most children remembered in fairly literal and concrete terms what they did with their parents. A 15-year-old girl whose mother had died said: "I think about the stupid little things we did together." A seven-year-old said, in remembering her father: "I think about all the things that he used to bring me and how he used to flip me over."

A few children reported that they still could not believe the death was real and sometimes forgot their parents had died. Others, reflecting on their new reality, thought about how hard it was to get along without their parents and wished for them to come back. Such reflections were painful and contrasted to the comforting memories that some children counseled a hypothetical bereaved child to call upon.

Linking Objects

Having an object belonging to the deceased was an important means of maintaining a link to him or her. *Linking objects,* a term used by Volkan (1981), refers to an aspect of the relationship or an object from that relationship that keeps the mourner living in the past. A more positive link or connection can be found in the concept of transitional objects—those that connect one realm of experience with another (Winnicott, 1953; Worden, 1991). These transitional objects provide comfort while one is engaged in the initial mourning process. Of the 125 children, 95 (77%) had something personal that belonged to their dead parents. They acquired these objects in different ways. Often it was something the deceased had given them or something belonging to the deceased that the child had taken after the death. Sometimes their surviving parents had given the objects to them or told them they could take what they wanted from the deceased parents' possessions. For the most part the children kept these items either on their person or in their rooms. One teenage girl said: "It makes me feel good to wear his shirt to school." Another girl said: "I carry his key chain; it makes me feel good . . . the way some people use crystals or whatever."

As the first year of mourning progressed, some of these transitional objects became less powerful for the children and took on more of the characteristics of "keepsakes" (Worden, 1991). A 13-year-old boy took his father's baseball hat and his cologne right after he learned that the father was dead. He did not understand why he did so, but he just reached out and took what was there and put it in his room. A year later both objects were still in his room. The hat now hung in a remote corner, rather than on the bedpost. Two years after the death, the boy was not sure what had happened to the hat. However, he said that he was reassured by his feeling that his father was always with him, making sure that "I am safe and stuff."

Role of the Surviving Parent

As was noted earlier, the authors see the process of constructing a connection to the deceased as part of an ongoing family dialogue. Not every parent was prepared to talk about the deceased, however. One father, who was primarily concerned with keeping his family going, remarked that his children had forgotten how often they were angry with their mother for being so involved outside the home. He acknowledged that he would listen to the children, but had little patience for their reminiscences. These children finally discovered that they could talk with each other about their mother and thus felt less frustrated with their father's silence.

On the other hand, some parents were eager to talk, but were met with resistance from the children. As one boy said, "I know my father would listen, but I don't want to talk." One year later, the boy remarked: "Talking makes me sad, but it is better than thinking about it alone. My father listens, and it really helps."

A ten-year-old boy whose sadness was clear and who could not talk about his father told the interviewer that his mother helped him to develop a positive memory of his father:

> She says we'll pray every night for Daddy and that he'll be able to see me. She says we have to remember Daddy outside in the sunshine laughing, not like he looked when he died. I asked if Daddy can help me now, if he'll always be with me. Mom said yes.

The children seemed to be comforted by being reminded of their dead parents, even when such reminders did not come from direct conversations with their surviving parents. Although he did not share his reaction with his mother, one 14-year-old commented: "It makes me feel good when I hear my mother talking to someone about how nice my father was."

Changes Over Time

By the second interview, some children who initially had reported no relevant dreams and who seemed to have little or no connection with the deceased found it easier to remember. An 11-year-old girl reported during the first interview that she did not dream about her mother, and she could not describe her to the interviewer. She was unable to concentrate at school because of her thoughts about her mother's absence. She did not possess anything that had belonged to her mother. Her sadness was palpable. She could not talk about her feelings, and she did not feel close to anyone in the family with whom she could talk about her mother.

By the end of the first year, this girl began to dream. She wanted to keep the dreams private, but said they went back to before her mother died. She visited the cemetery, where she talked to her mother; in her head, she could hear her mother's voice, giving her good advice. She took some of her mother's jewelry and kept it in her room. Her schoolwork improved, and her sadness seemed less pervasive. She talked to her friends and her father about her mother and what her mother was like:

> This Christmas was hard, but I got through it because I got used to it. Just looking at her picture is hard because I miss her. I think about whether or not she can see me and she can hear me. Is she happy? I hear her voice in my head telling me it's OK. I talk to my friends I can trust and to my dad because he loved her, too, and understands what I am going through.

It is not clear if this girl was better able to confront the loss and tolerate sad feelings because she found a way of connecting with her deceased mother or if being able to tolerate her feelings enabled her to connect with her mother.

Discussion

This paper has described an aspect of the bereavement process in children: the establishment of a set of memories, feelings, and actions that the authors have called "constructing" the deceased. This inner representation or construction leads the child to remain in a relationship with the deceased, and this relationship changes as the child matures and as the intensity of the grief lessens. The concept of identification is insufficient to describe what was observed. A child may construct a sense of the deceased and develop an inner representation of that person that does not involve (at either a conscious or an unconscious level) becoming like that person. Memorializing, remembering, and knowing who died are active processes that may continue throughout the child's entire life. Rubin (1985) noted that there seems to be a relationship between the comfort and fluidity with which the bereaved can relate to the representations of the deceased and their ability to cope effectively with the loss. Although the intensity of the relationship with the deceased must diminish with time, it does not disappear. This is not a matter of living in the past, but rather recognizing how the past informs the present.

These findings suggest a shift in our understanding of the bereavement process. Bereavement should not be viewed as a psychological state that ends or from which one recovers. The intensity of feelings may lessen and the child may become oriented more to the future than to the past, but a concept of closure that requires a determination of when the bereavement process ends does not seem compatible with the view suggested by these findings. The emphasis should be on negotiating and renegotiating the meaning of the loss over time, rather than on letting go. While the loss is permanent and unchanging, the process is not. Thus bereavement should be understood as a cognitive, as well as an emotional, process that takes place in a social context of which the deceased is a part.

Children's cognitive processes include their ability to experience complex feeling states, as well as their inborn qualities and their intellectual and social development. Piaget (1954) observed that development involves a push toward greater mastery of one's situation, in Kegan's view (1982), mastery emerges as children construct and reconstruct their world to find greater coherence and new meanings that can unify memories and feelings into a temporary coherent whole that prevails until the child moves to the next stage of development. The ability to call up memories of specific events; abstractions concerning the nature of past interactions: and on the highest level, descriptions of the deceased's personality, likes, and dislikes depends on the child's level of development.

Accommodation may be a more suitable term than *recovery*, or *closure* for what takes place as a result of a death in the family. However, in this context, accommodation should not be viewed as a static phenomenon. Rather, it is a continuing set of activities—related both to others and to shifting self-perceptions as the child's mind and body change—that affect the way the child constructs meaning. In this process, the child seeks to gain not only an understanding of the meaning of death, but a sense of the meaning of this now-dead parent in his or her life. To do so requires the development of a common language for talking about the death and the person who died.

When an experience is recreated in language, it may lose in immediacy, but it is more likely to be kept in memory. Critical to representation in language is the family's use of ritual that could legitimate the construction of an inner representation of the deceased. Most non-Western cultures have rituals that help their members acknowledge and cope with loss and with the sense of the deceased (Rosenblatt, Walsh, & Jackson, 1976; Silverman & Silverman, 1979). The need for such rituals is acknowledged less in contemporary

146 ◆ Children Mourning, Mourning Children

Western thinking and worldviews. We may need to look anew at rituals that facilitate dialogue and other kinds of relationships to the past.

The interview data reported in this paper have identified ways in which the child maintains a connection to the deceased parent. These data challenge the traditional clinical practice of encouraging the bereaved to disengage from the deceased. In facilitating mourning, those who work with children may need to focus on how to transform connections and place the relationship in a new perspective, rather than on how to separate from the deceased.

References

Anderson. R. (1974) Notes of a survivor. In S.B. Troop & W.A. Green (Eds.). *The patient, death and the family* (pp. 73-82). New York: Charles Scribner's Sons.

Bowlby, J. (1980). *Attachment and loss: Vol. 3. Loss, sadness, and depression.* New York: Basic Books.

Dietrich, D.R., & Shabad, P.C. (1989). *The problem of loss and mourning.* Madison, CT: International Universities Press.

Freud, S. (1957). Mourning and melancholia. In J. Strachey (Ed. and Trans.), *The standard edition of the complete psychological works of Sigmund Freud* (Vol. 14. pp. 237-258). London: Hogarth Press. (Original work published 1917)

Furman, E. (1974). *A child's parent dies: Studies in childhood bereavement.* New Haven, CT: Yale University Press.

Furman, E. (1984). Children's patterns in mourning the death of a loved one. In H. Wass & C. Corr (Eds.), *Childhood and death* (pp- 185-203). Washington, DC: Hemisphere Publishing.

Gergen, K.J. (1985). The social constructionist movement in modern psychology. *American Psychologist, 40,* 266-273.

Glaser, B., & Strauss, A. (1967). *The discovery of grounded theory.* Chicago: Aldine Publishing.

Jacobs, S.C., Koston, T.R., Dasl, S., & Ostfeld, A-M. (1987). Attachment theory and multiple dimensions of grief. *Omega. 18,* 41-52.

Jacobson, E. (1965). The return of the lost parent. In M. Schur (Ed.), *Drives, affects, and behaviors* (Vol. 2, pp. 193-211). New York: International Universities Press.

Kegan, R. (1982). *The evolving self: Problem and process in human development.* Cambridge, MA: Harvard University Press.

Klass, D. (1988). *Parental grief: Solace and resolution.* New York: Springer.

Lifton, R.J. (1979). *The broken connection: On death and the continuity of life.* New York: Simon & Schuster.

Lonetto, R. (1980). *Children's conceptions of death* (Vol. 3). New York: Springer.

Miller, J.B.M. (1971). Children's reactions to the death of a parent: A review of the psychoanalytic literature. *Journal of the American Psychoanalytic Association, 19,* 697-719.

Moss, M.S., & Moss, S.Z. (1981). The image of the deceased spouse in remarriage of elderly widowers. *Journal of Gerontological of Social Work, 3*(2), 59-70.

Nickman, S.L. 1985). Loss in adoption: The importance of dialogue. *Psychoanalytic Study of the Child, 40,* 365-398.

Osterweis, M., Solomon, F., & Greene, M. (Eds.). (1984). *Bereavement: Reactions, consequences, and care.* Washington, DC: National Academy Press.

Piaget, J. (1954). *The construction of reality in the child* (M. Cook Trans.). New York: Basic Books.

Rizzuto, A.M. (1979). *The birth of the living God: A psychoanalytic study.* Chicago: University of Chicago Press.

Rochlin, G. (1959). Loss and restitution. *Psychoanalytic Study of the Child, 8,* 288-309.

Rochlin, G. (1965). *Griefs and discontents: The forces of change.* Boston: Little, Brown.

Rosenblatt, P., & Elde, C. (1990). Shared reminiscence about a deceased parent: Implications for grief education and grief counselling. *Family Relations, 39,*206-210.

Rosenblatt, P.C., Walsh, R.P., & Jackson, D.A. (1976). *Grief and mourning in cross-cultural perspective* [Machine-readable data file]. Human Relations Area Files.

Rubin, S.S. (1985). The resolution of bereavement: A clinical focus on the relationship to the deceased. *Psychotherapy: Theory, Research, Training and Practice, 22*, 231-235.

Schafer, R. (1968). *Aspects of internalization.* New York: International Universities Press.

Silverman, P.R. (1986). *Widow to widow.* New York: Springer.

Silverman, P.R. (1989). The impact of the death of a parent on college age women. *Psychiatric Clinics of North America, 10*, 387-404.

Silverman, P.R., & Worden, J.W. (1992). Children's

reactions to the death of a parent in the early months after the death. *American Journal of Orthopsychiatry, 62*, 93-104.

Silverman, S.M., & Silverman, P.R. (1979). Parent-child communication in widowed families. *American Journal of Psychotherapy, 33*, 428-441.

Smilansky, S. (1987). *On death: Helping children understand and cope.* New York: Peter Lang.

Strauss, A.L. (1987). *Qualitative analysis for social scientists.* Cambridge, England: Cambridge University Press.

Volkan, V.D. (1981). *Linking objects and linking phenomena.* New York: International Universities Press.

Weisman, A. (1972). *On dying and denying: A psychiatric study of terminality.* New York: Behavioral Publications.

Winnicott, D.W. (1953). Transitional objects and transitional phenomena. *International Journal of Psychoanalysis, 34*, 89-97.

Wolfenstein, M. (1973). The image of the lost parent.

Psychoanalytic Study of the Child, 28, 433-456.

Worden, J.W. (1991). *Grief counseling and grief therapy: A handbook for the mental health practitioner* (2nd ed.). New York: Springer.

The Empty Space Phenomenon: The Process of Grief in the Bereaved Family

12

S. G. McClowry, E. B. Davies, K. A. May, E. J. Kulenkamp, and I. M. Martinson

Forty-nine families who experienced a death following childhood cancer were interviewed 7-9 years after the death. Interviews were analyzed using grounded theory technique for qualitative data for the purpose of examining the long-term responses of families to childhood death. In contrast to bereavement theories which claim that grief is usually resolved within two years, findings of this study suggest that many parents and siblings still experience pain and loss after 7-9 years. Analysis suggests that the death of a child creates an "empty space" for surviving family members. Three patterns of grieving were described by family members in response to this sense of emptiness: "getting over it," "filling the emptiness," and "keeping the connection." Differences and similarities of these patterns are enumerated. The perceived significance of the relationship to the pattern of grief is hypothesized. Situations which stimulate a recurrence or continuation of the "empty space" are suggested and changes over time in the bereavement process are described. Further research implications are proposed.

Introduction

Current bereavement theory describes grief as a series of hierarchical steps leading to resolution if the death is accepted or to pathological grief if intense grief reactions are continued longer than expected. Lindemann's study of grief (1) was among the earliest in bereavement research. He concluded that grief reactions should be completed within weeks of the death of a loved one. Others (2, 3)

Funded by the California Division, American Cancer Society, Grant No. 2-210-PR-14, Ida M. Martinson, RN, PhD, Principal Investigator.

propose up to one year for the nearly complete diminishment of distress symptoms.

While most of the earlier literature claims that grief is something that can be resolved or completed, clinical experience indicates that for many bereaved, resolution does not occur by one year. Indeed, as the Committee for the Study of Health Consequences of the Stress of Bereavement states (4), for some individuals the pain of loss may continue for a lifetime even when there is successful adaptation.

A limitation of much of the past bereavement research is the time frame in which data are collected. Most studies focus on the period immediately after a death or up to two years after the loss. In order to study the process of grief in the bereaved families, a lengthier longitudinal approach seemed necessary. In 1976, Martinson began the Home Care for the Child with Cancer project in Minnesota (5-8). Fifty-eight children died during the two years of the project. Of the 58 families whose child died, 25 resided in the metropolitan St. Paul area, 25 in cities and rural areas throughout the state, and 8 in neighboring states. According to the Hollingshead (9) Two-Factor Index of Social Position, the families represented the entire socio-economic range of the index with concentration in the middle to lower income classes. One parent was of Latin descent, another Native American, the rest of the families were White.

In order to provide support to these families as well as to describe their grief process during the first two years, the families were followed after the death of their child and were interviewed at one month, six months, twelve months, and two years. The results of those studied are published elsewhere (10-12).

The Current Study

Returning to the same families, the current study involved interviews with the families 7-9 years after the death of their child. The purpose of this study was to describe what happens to families several years after experiencing a death from childhood cancer. Questions during the interview focused on the families' memories of their child's illness and death, their subsequent bereavement process, and the present life of the family members.

This large qualitative data set included interviews with 49 families, parents and siblings. Nine of the original 58 families did not participate for the following reasons: one family moved out of the country, one family could not be located, and seven declined. Family members agreeing to participate signed consent forms as approved by the Human Subjects Committee of the University of California, San Francisco.

Semistructured interviews, totaling 178 hours of transcribed audio-tape served as the primary data source. A total of 150 interviews were conducted with 46 mothers, 33 fathers/stepfathers, and 71 siblings. Of the parental interviews, 28 couples chose to be interviewed together. The mean age of the mothers participating in the current study was 44.4 years. Of the fathers, the mean age was 41.9 years which reflects the exclusion of four fathers who had died since their child's death. The total mean age of the siblings including those born or adopted since the child's death is 18.7 years. Of those siblings who were interviewed, the mean age was also 18.7.

During a preliminary reading of several of the transcribed interviews, two contradictions to the literature surfaced. First, the family responses suggested the time required for the bereavement process is indeed longer than a year or two. Even after 7-9 years, subjects were still expressing pain and loss. Secondly, rather than describing conditions which would suggest resolution, families were describing something different in the interviews; instead of "letting go" of the love one, families detailed the presence of an "empty space in their lives. Through comments like "There's always one missing" or "It doesn't seem right yet. I mean, it kind of seems almost empty, that part," they delineated a concept as yet undescribed by current bereavement theory and research.

The phenomenon of an "empty space" was intriguing and stimulated many other questions: Did all the families experience an empty space"? Was the "empty space" the end stage of grief or did the presence of the "empty space" surface over time? Could the "empty space" be explained as loneliness or depression? Might "the empty space" influence whether the families' lives continued in a productive and a happy manner? And finally, does every death cause an "empty space" or is this phenomenon specific to parental loss of a child or to a sibling death?

Analysis was undertaken to further examine this concept of "empty space" and likewise to see whether families actually experienced what is, according to the literature, believed to be the trajectory of grief responses. Since at the time of this insight, half of the interviews had not as yet been conducted, the following question was added to the interview guide to explore families's experiences in regard to a sense of emptiness: "Some people tell me that they have a continuing sense of emptiness or feel the presence of an 'empty space.' I'm not sure that's always true. What have you experienced?"

Methodology

The interview data were analyzed using grounded theory technique for qualitative data (13, 14). Grounded theory methodology is a systematic research approach for the collection and analysis of qualitative data (15). The method is appropriate for research use when the phenomenon studied has undergone little empirical examination and requires an exploratory descriptive method (14). Data are subjected to a systematic constant comparative analysis for recurrent themes and concepts (13, 14). As patterns in the data suggest interrelationships, the researcher hypothesizes connections between the categories which are revised or eliminated through continued comparisons (16). Propositions are generated which reflect the interrelationships of concepts as described by the participants. Finally hypotheses are proposed in the form of substantive theory and may be used to guide further research of the phenomenon (17).* Grounded theory methodology has been applied to the topic of death and bereavement by several researchers (18-20). By using this method, family bereavement theory can be extended while remaining grounded in the actual experiences reported by the family members during their interviews.

Findings

While the initial loss of the child appeared to create an "empty space" for family members, further analysis of the data suggested three patterns of grieving in response to this feeling of emptiness. In one pattern of grief, "getting over it" was the recurrent theme. In another pattern, reports of methods used for "filling the emptiness" predominated the interviews. But in the third pattern, "keeping the

---

*A comprehensive explanation of ground theory methodology is beyond the scope of the paper. For further information about the technique and other examples of research which have applied this technique, the reader is advised to read the articles by K. A. May which are cited in the references.

connection" was important to those who continued to experience the sense of loss or "empty space."

Getting Over It

Family members who did not continue to experience the "empty space" could be described as those who resolved their grief in the traditional sense of "getting over it." They did not describe their grief in an intense manner. The individuals who talked about "getting over it" accepted the death matter-of-factly as either God's will or as one father explained:

> I used to sit down with the kids after he died and say, "We have to try and lead a normal life. Death is something we have to face. We've all got to die sometime, you know. It's a thing that happens."

When asked how the death affected theirs lives, the people who succeeded in "getting over it" stated they did not think it had any effect on their current life. Instead, they said the death happened long ago so they did not remember much anymore. The memories of the people who were able to "get over with it" were less vivid than the other two groups.

Filling the Emptiness

Rather than "getting over it," the second group attempted to "fill the emptiness" in one of two ways: by "keeping busy" or by substituting other problems or situations to take their mind off their grief. One family built a new home immediately after the death of their child and spent all their energy working on the house. Another adopted their single daughter's baby who was born soon after their son died. A few increased their food or alcohol intake. Others had new babies or adopted other children. Returning to work, school, or beginning a new goal were ways this group utilized to "fill the emptiness." Another way was taking on the religious beliefs of the deceased child or exploring their own spirituality.

In yet another family, all members described tremendous marital problems resulting in a bitter divorce. The family members in the divorced family did not express a great deal of pain with the death but focused in the interview on the problems associated with the marital stress. As the adult son in the divorced family described his mother's response to her son's death:

> She really doesn't talk about it. She seems to be ok, you know. She doesn't mope around or hate the world for it. She's got other problems to worry about and that takes her mind off it.

Others attempted to "fill the emptiness" by "keeping busy" through altruistic involvements. Some became involved in grief work through church groups, Candlelighters (a support group for the parents of children with cancer), or organizations focused on other children's causes such as caring for abused or for retarded children. At least for a while, it seemed important for these people to use their experiences by getting involved with families in similar situations. They appeared to need to have some good evolve from the pain of losing someone they loved. In so doing, they were able to reduce their own sense of loss. As one mother said when she was asked if she had a continuing sense of emptiness.

> No. I can't say I do. I think that is why I filled up all that emptiness with others kids.

Those choosing to "fill the emptiness" with altruistic involvements eventually described a change in their attitude toward the work they were doing. Whether to redirect their energies in another way or to complete their participation, they felt the need to go beyond where they were as if the emptiness was for the most part filled. One of the mothers explained:

> You don't forget it, you know. Regarding my work in Candlelighters, I don't want to do it anymore. I don't want to be a parent anymore who had a child with cancer. It doesn't mean I don't identify or feel for it; but that used to be my identity. If you didn't know that about me, you didn't know me. And now, I don't feel that anymore. I feel that I have something else to me. I'm not me just because my child died of cancer. I want to broaden out. There's something else out there.

Keeping the Connection

Many of the people who continued to be aware of an "empty space" were, in fact, involved in activities which "filled the emptiness" for others, such as moving to a new home or becoming involved in support groups for bereaved parents. However, instead of "filling the emptiness" these individuals described a continuing sense of their loss. One father contrasts the differences in his pattern of "keeping the connection" with his wife's ability to "feel the emptiness":

> Connie certainly launched into Candlelighters. I don't think I would have had that energy. It would have taken me a whole lot longer. She was more ready to channel her energies into something that seemed related to Brian and I couldn't.

Rather than "getting over it," the people who demonstrated this pattern integrated their pain and loss into their lives. In contrast to "letting go" like the people who had "gotten over it," this group had vivid memories and stories to report which they did not want to forget. Instead they cherished their recollections, and saw "keeping the connection" as desirable as reflected in statements like this one:

> We'll never forget. She's with us to this day. And it isn't always bad. We had a lot of good times with her too. She was funny. So it isn't always sad or upsetting to talk or think about her.

Eventually, even though still "keeping the connection," two changes occurred in those demonstrating this pattern of grief. First, the intensity of pain experienced when thinking or talking about the deceased child gradually lessened. Then, following the reduction in pain was a desire for something else on which to focus their energy. There was a great deal of variation in the length of time which passed before the pain become comfortable and, in fact, comforting. However, a commonly described benchmark by the families was wanting something new in their lives, not to replace the loss of the child or to "fill the emptiness," but to stimulate interest in the present:

> After a while, we went through a bad time. We were having all kinds of trouble. We weren't arguing or anything, but we just didn't have anything to get us going. It was the reason we built this house. It kind of gave us a goal in our life. It got us together to make some more decisions. I think it helped us and we enjoy the house. I think the change was good for us.

Another family talked about how they proceeded to add some sparkle to their family:

> Two years after Lisa died it seemed that the kids were still afraid to have fun. There was a long period where we felt like we couldn't

smile. It just seemed like something was missing. I told Peter, "You know, what we need around here is a dog." So we picked out this dog and he's been just like a member of the family. The kids started playing with the dog and he brought them out of their shell. I think the dog really got us so we could laugh.

Although most of the individuals who were "keeping the connection" expressed satisfaction with their present lives, they continue to reserve a small part of themselves for the loss of a special relationship which they view as irreplaceable. As one mother explained:

> At times, it's this emptiness. Scars are always, always there. Part of that I don't ever want to lose because I feel connected.

Significance of the Relationship to Pattern of Grieving

A possible association between the significance of the relationship to the deceased and the desire to "keep the connection" was explored. During the interviews, family members were asked whether they experienced other deaths and how they reacted. By comparing and contrasting their descriptions, it appeared that the pattern of grieving was associated with the perceived quality of the relationships. Those who described the deceased person in terms of a particular relationship irreplaceable by anyone or anything experienced a continuing "empty space." In contrast, the same people might describe the death of others as a loss but not with the intensity of the loss of those whose death became an "empty space." For example, one of the teenaged siblings also experienced the death of three grandparents since her sister's death. Two of those grandparents are spoken about in the manner similar to the "empty space" she experienced from her sister's death; the other grandparent's death appeared to cause little distress. Even among the siblings' descriptions of each other, not all relationships were valued equally. For some children, the grief response was not as intense if they did not view themselves as close to the dying sibling as they were to another brother or sister. One sister said about the death of her brother Terry:

> I don't think it was so bad for me because it was me and Paul and then there's my sister and Terry together. So I still had my older brother.

In contrast, another teen who had a remaining sister still described an "empty space" from the death of her older sister.

> I don't think I'll ever get over it because it really bothers me. Andrea and I are eight years apart, but Jennifer and I were only three years apart. I miss the closeness of a sister that age. It's not bumming me out. I'm not depressed about it. It's just she'd understand. You can't always go to your parents about some things. You can go to a friend, but a sister would be more confidential. I miss that a lot.

Recurrences of the Empty Space

While those who "keep the connection" have a continuing sense of an "empty space," those who "filled the emptiness" have periodic times when the "empty space" is likely to emerge. One of these times is when asked how many children are in the family. Parents and siblings reported that responding is difficult since the question is asked by new acquaintances who are not aware that the family lost a child. They answered by either including the deceased child in their numerical response without any further explanation, or by adding that there was also a child who died or just stating the number of living children but feeling uncomfortable as if they were excluding or ignoring the deceased child.

Answering "how many children" was particular painful for the mother who lost her only child:

> People will say, "Do you have children?" If I say no that puts me in a different role because that makes me a child-free person who has never known parenthood.

Holidays and anniversary dates like the child's birthdate or death were described as particularly difficult times for the families when the "empty space" feeling would be more constant and painful, although the intensity of this feeling decreased with time. One mother also said gatherings with the extended family were dreaded because she knew people would notice that one of her children was missing. Likewise, family portraits were uncomfortable. One describes her mother's reaction:

> It will never be the same. Even little things like getting a family portrait. Mother has never wanted to. We get family pictures at weddings but there is a sense still that it's not complete. Despite

the fact that Tom, Jim, and I are married and have kids and different things going on, there's still a sense of not everybody being there.

Changes Over Time

The process of grief described by the families changes over time. How this occurs is associated with the pattern of grief demonstrated.

For those who describe "getting over it," time brings a cessation of pain and a desire to go on with life as it is now. They do not view themselves as significantly changed by the death. Instead they make a conscious effort to put the experiences of the child's life and death in the past.

In a different manner, those who attempted to "fill the emptiness," still periodically experience an "empty space." However, they continue to concentrate on the parts of their current lives which they view as important.

For those "keeping the connection," the interviews suggest that the sense of emptiness continues but changes over time. How this occurs is explained by one mother who at an interview two weeks after the death said, "I am as aware of his absence as I was of his presence during his life." During the interview nine years after her son's death, the same mother went on to clarify how the emptiness evolved:

> The constant pain was unbearable but we bore it. And I don't know which was worse, that or when it let it up a bit and something would trigger it unexpectedly, and unexpected seemed to be worse than when the pain was constant. You know, turn a corner and see something and wow! . . . when you just weren't thinking about it and then pow! here it comes again.

> We moved things out of his room . . . probably much too soon. Then we had a hole that kept moving within that house. Because his room was empty, we put some bookcases and things in there from the living room so it wouldn't be an empty room. Then that end of the living room was empty. So we moved a picture down from upstairs and then there was a hole upstairs. I mean, we moved the absence. . . all the way around, and there was no getting rid of it. And if you bought something new, it would have been to fill the hole. You know, there was just no way to cope with the fact that he's missing . . . that Tommy's missing and his presence in our house, his little furniture and everything was missing.

> There is an emptiness still. I haven't found anything that would substitute or fill it, but it's receded. The emptiness is within me now instead of that empty arm feeling.

Although many of the individuals "keeping the connection" described their current lives as productive acid happy, and although they have over the intervening 7-9 years experienced various changes which would indicate continued growth and development such as beginning new jobs or being promoted, having other children, and enjoying new or renewed recreational activities, there was also a qualitative change as they integrated the loss into their lives. A few of the deaths resulted in bitterness and distrust, but for most the loss was eventually seen as an incentive to cherish other significant relationships and treasure daily events as a special gift.

In addition, those "keeping the connection" found that eventually the pain was no longer restricting and preoccupying. Time lessened their pain until it became a comfortable pain filled with memories which they did not want to forget. Opportunities to "keep the connection" even after 7-9 years were still desired as explained by one of the brothers who described how he felt when visiting his sister's grave:

> It bothers me to go because it keeps reminding me that she's not here. But when I do go, it also makes me feel good. It makes me feel like she's close again. I believe in God and I believe she's in heaven. But still I feel her spirit and I get warmer inside. She and I were real close.

Summary

This explanatory study suggests that families who have experienced a death from childhood cancer feel a sense of emptiness or an "empty space" after the death of their child. Based on the analysis presented, there appear to be three different patterns of grieving: "getting over it," "filling the emptiness," and "keeping the connection." Whether the family members continued to experience an "empty space" was associated with their willingness and/or ability to either "get over it" or "fill the emptiness." Those who did neither continued to experience an "empty space" even after 7-9 years. This allowed them to "keep the connection" which they viewed as desirous. Similarly, even after 7-9 years, those who "filled the emptiness," periodically experienced an "empty space" in situations which emphasized the missingness of the deceased child. However, the activities which they used to "fill the emptiness" predominated their current lives. In contrast, those whose grief pattern was "getting over it," viewed the death as a past event which did not significantly influence their current lives.

Limitations

The aim of grounded theory methodology is the discovery of theory (13, 14). This proposed theory of family bereavement, based on what the families have described about their process of grief marks a dramatic departure from the literature on bereavement. What is proposed is a substantive theory based on empirical data (14) and is categorized as exploratory research.

Future examination of the phenomenon of the "empty space" and patterns of grieving will determine the validity of this theory. Validity will particularly be determined in clinical situations when the reports of those who have experienced the death of a child will either validate or refute what is proposed. Also, the examination of other groups of bereaved families and those grieving different losses, such as spousal death will add further to the understanding of this phenomenon.

These findings may hold implications for those who work with bereaved individuals. However, suggesting interventions based on these results may be premature due to the level of understanding of this phenomenon. However, these finding can serve to sensitize care providers to the patterns the bereaved family members may utilize.

Based on the experiences reported by the 49 families in this study, it does appears that grief is an individual journey that should not be expected to follow time limits and a specific path. Rather than suggesting interventions which help bereaved individuals in "getting over it," "filling the emptiness," "keeping the connection," this study merely describes the differences in patterns of those who are grieving the loss of a child from cancer. No pattern of grieving is suggested as superior to the others. However, bereavement counselors may recognize the potential difficulty of family members to share their grief with each other when different patterns are used by individuals in the family. Instead, understanding that people often respond differently to grief may facilitate family communication and mutual support.

Until more is known about these patterns, continuing to listen, care, and accept what the bereaved describe will add to the understanding of the process of grief. In addition, those people who continue to feel a sense of emptiness and pain after two years can be assured that they are not alone.

References

1. Lindemann, E. (1944). Symptomatology and management of acute grief. *American Journal of Psychiatry,* 101, 141-149.
2. Mawson, D., Marks, I., Ramm, L., & Stern, R. (1981). Guided mourning for morbid grief: A controlled study. *British Journal of Psychiatry,* 138, 185-193.
3. Ramsay, R. W. (1979). Bereavement: A behavioral treatment of pathological grief. In P. O. Sjoden, S. Bates, and W. S. Dorkens, III (Eds.), *Trends in Behavior Therapy.* New York: Academic Press.
4. Osterweis, M., Solomon, F., & Green, M. (Eds.). (1984). *Bereavement: Reactions, consequences, and care.* Washington, DC: National Academy Press.
5. Martinson, I. M. (1985). *The bereaved family.* 1985 Pediatric Hospice Conference Report, 60-61.
6. Martinson, I. M., Armstrong, G., Geis, D., Anglim, M., Gronseth, E., McInnis, H., Nesbit, M., & Kersey, J. (1978a). Facilitating home care for children dying of cancer. *Cancer Nursing,* 1, 41-45.
7. Martinson, I. M., Armstrong, G., Geis, D., Anglim, M., Gronseth, E., McInnis, H., Nesbit, M., & Kersey, J. (1978b). Home care for children dying of cancer. *Pediatrics,* 62, 106-113.
8. Moldow, D., & Martinson, I. M. (1980). From research to reality: Home care for the dying child. *The American Journal of Maternal-Child Nursing,* 51, 159-166.
9. Hollingshead, A. B. (1957). *The two-factor index of social position.* Author published.
10. Martinson, I. M., Moldow, D. G., Armstrong, G. D., Henry, W. F., Nesbit, M. E., & Kersey, J. H. (1986). Home care for children dying of cancer. *Research in Nursing and Health,* 9, 11-16.
11. Martinson, I., Nesbitt, M., & Kersey, J. (In press). Children's adjustment to the death of a sibling from cancer. *Journal of Thanatology.*

12. Smith, C., Garvis, M., & Martinson, I. (1983). Content analysis of interviews using a nursing model: A look at parents adapting to the impact of childhood cancer. *Cancer Nursing, 6*(4), 269-275.
13. Glaser, B. (1978). *Theoretical sensitivity.* Mill Valley, CA: The Sociology Press.
14. Glaser, B., & Strauss, A. (1967a). *The discovery of ground theory, strategies for qualitative research.* Chicago: Aldine.
15. Chenitz, W. C., & Swanson, J., M. (1986). *From practice to grounded theory.* Menlo Park, CA: Addison-Wesley.
16. May, K. A. (1980). A typology of detachment/involvement patterns adopted during pregnancy by first-time expectant fathers. *Western Journal of Nursing Research, 2,* 445-461.
17. May, K. A. (1982). Three phases of father involvement in pregnancy. *Nursing Research, 31*(6), 337-342.
18. Benoliel, J. Q. (1967). *The nurse and the dying patient.* New York: Macmillan.
19. Glaser, B., & Strauss, A. (1965). *Awareness of dying.* Chicago: Aldine.
20. Glaser, B., & Strauss, A. (1967b). *Time for dying.* Chicago: Aldine.

A Sampler of Literature for Young Readers: Death, Dying, and Bereavement

Charles A. Corr

1) Picture books for very young people; mostly about animals:

Margaret Wise Brown, *The Dead Bird*. Reading, MA: Addison-Wesley, 1958. Extremely simple text and pictures for very young readers. Straightforward story line about finding a wild bird that is dead, touching it, burying it, and mourning it ("until they forgot"). An early classic. AV

Carol Carrick, *The Accident*. NY: Seabury, 1976. Christopher's dog, Bodger, is killed in an accident when he runs in front of a truck. The boy is angry (and, in part, guilty). His parents bury Bodger too quickly, before he can take part. But he and his father can erect a marker at Bodger's grave. AV

Edith T. Hurd, *The Black Dog Who Went into the Woods*. NY: Harper & Row, 980. Family members react to the death of their dog; each has a dream.

Mildred Kantrowitz, *When Violet Died*. NY: Parents' Magazine Press, 1973. The death of Amy and Eva's pet bird is followed by a funeral involving their friends and sadness at the realization that nothing lasts forever. But Eva realizes that life can go on through the family cat, Blanche, and its kittens.

Judith Liberman, *The Bird's Last Song*. Reading, MA: Addison-Wesley, 1976. When migratory birds come back from winter in the south they hear the thawing melody of the old bird's last (frozen) song. Lovely woodcuts.

Edith G. Stull, *My Turtle Died Today*. NY: Holt, Rinehart & Winston, 1964. A boy seeks help for his dying turtle. It dies and is mourned. Life goes on through Patty's kittens. Can you get a new mother? Do you have to live—a long time—before you die? AV

Judith Viorst, *The Tenth Good Thing about Barney*. NY: Atheneum, 1971. Barney, the boy's cat, dies, is buried, and is mourned. How to write a eulogy? Barney was: brave and smart and funny and clean; and cuddly and handsome and he only once ate a bird; it was sweet to hear him purr in my ear, and sometimes he slept on my belly and kept it warm. But that's only 9. Are cats in heaven? The 10th good thing is learned in the garden: Barney is in the ground and he's helping the flowers to grow.

Sandol S. Warburg, *Growing Time.* Boston: Houghton Mifflin, 1969. A boy and his aging Collie, King. New puppy at the end?

Hans Wilhelm, *I'll Always Love You.* NY: Crown, 1985. A boy and his dog, Elfie. Regrets that they didn't tell her that they loved her, but the boy did each night.

2) More for young children; about grandparents:

Jennifer Bartoli, *Nonna.* NY: Harvey House, 1975. A boy and his younger sister have good memories of being with Grandma on her swing and of her cookies. They are involved in her funeral, burial, and settling her affairs.

Tommie de Paola, *Nana Upstairs and Nana Downstairs.* NY: Putnam, 1973. Tommy likes to visit his grandmother and his great-grandmother (with whom he plays and shares, including being restrained in a chair). Nana Upstairs dies; he sees a falling star and is comforted that it is a kiss from Nana who is now "upstairs" in a new way. Later, both Nanas are "upstairs."

Joan Fassler, *My Grandpa Died Today.* NY: Human Sciences Press, 1971. David copes with the sudden, natural death of his grandfather, even as he is comforted by flashbacks to the many good memories of their relationship. AV ("The Day Grandpa Died")

Audrey Harris, *Why Did He Die?* Minneapolis: Lerner, 1965. A mother explains death to her young son whose friend's grandfather has died. Question and answer format; aging, the life cycle, memories, quality of life.

Barbara S. Hazen, *Why Did Grandpa Die? A Book about Death.* NY: Golden, 1985. Young Molly and her grandfather have much in common. When Grandpa dies suddenly, Molly cannot accept this harsh fact and does not feel like crying. Her father reminds her that Grandpa was also his father whom he loved very much. Many things remind Molly of how much she misses Grandpa. It takes a long time to acknowledge that he will not come back.

Miska Miles, *Annie and the Old One.* Boston: Little, Brown, 1971. A 10-year-old Navajo girl is told that when her mother finishes weaving a rug it will be time for grandmother to return to Mother Earth. Annie tries to unravel the weaving in secret and to distract her mother from weaving, until the adults realize what is going on and her grandmother explains that we are all part of a natural cycle. When Annie realizes that she cannot hold back time, she is ready to learn to weave. AV

Linda Peavy, *Allison's Grandfather.* NY: Chas. Scribner's Sons, 1981. Erica thinks about his friend's grandfather (on his ranch) while he is dying. Momma holds his hand as he dies.

Charlotte Zolotow, *My Grandson Lew*. NY: Harper, 1974. Lewis awakens in the night and wonders why his grandfather has not visited recently. The mother had not told her son that the grandfather is dead because he hadn't asked. The boy says that he hadn't needed to ask; his grandfather just came. They share warm memories of someone they both miss, e.g., "he gave me eye hugs." "Now we will remember him together and neither of us will be so lonely as we would be if we had to remember him alone." (Loss shared is eased.) AV

3) Still for younger readers; about trees:

Leo Buscaglia, *The Fall of Freddy the Leaf*. Thorofare, NJ: Slack, 1982. Freddy and other leaves discuss their fall from the tree.

Alvin Tresselt, *The Dead Tree*. NY: Parent's Magazine Press. Description of a tree and its roles at different stages in its life cycle.

4) Books about the death of a peer or the death of a parent:

Andrea F. Clardy, *Dusty Was My Friend: Coming to Terms with Loss*. Human Sciences, 1984. Benjamin (8) remembers his friend Dusty (10), who was killed in a car accident, and tries to understand his feelings about losing a friend in this way.

Janice Cohn, *I Had a Friend Named Peter*. NY: Wm. Morrow, 1987. Beth's friend, Peter, is killed by a car; her parents & teacher answer questions.

Jean Little, *Mama's Going to Buy You a Mockingbird*. NY: Viking Kestrel, 1984. Jeremy and his younger sister, Sarah, only learn that their father is dying from cancer by overhearing someone talking about it. Lack of information and limited contacts when he is in the hospital leave the children confused and angry. Two central themes in this story are: the many losses, large and small, that accompany dying and death; and the need for support from others.

E. Sandy Powell, *Geranium Morning*. Minneapolis: CarolRhoda Books, 1990. This is the story of two young children: Timothy, whcse father died suddenly in an accident, and Frannie, whose mother is dying. The children struggle with strong feelings, memories, guilt ("if onlys"), and some unhelpful adult actions. But they also are helped by Frannie's father and by her mother before she dies. Above all, in sharing their losses, the two children help each other.

Joan S. Prestine, *Someone Special Died*. LA: Price/Stern/Sloan, 1987. Attitudes in grief; memories.

Doris Sanford, *It Must Hurt a Lot*. Portland, OR: Multnomah Press, 1986. Anya's reactions to a death and realizations (secrets) about what such reactions teach.

5) Books that explain grief and/or funeral practices:

Caroline Arnold, *What We Do When Someone Dies*. NY: Franklin Watts, 1987. Explains funeral customs & memorialization ceremonies.

Elizabeth Adam Corley, *Tell Me about Death, Tell Me about Funerals*. Santa Clara, CA: Grammatical Sciences, 1973. A funeral director describes a conversation between her father and a young girl whose grandfather has recently died. Topics include gu~lt, abandonment, and especially choices about funerals, burial, cemeteries, mausoleums, etc. I especially like mention of the "polarbears" who carry the casket.

Marge Heegard, *When Someone Very Special Dies*. Minneapolis: Woodland, 1988. A story line for children to illustrate or color.

Phyllis Rash Hughes, *Dying is Different*. Mahomet, IL: Mech Mentor, 1978. A read-together book: depictions of life and of death on alternate pages, plus some lessons to learn and guidance for share.

Joy and Marv Johnson, *Tell Me, Papa: A Family Book for Children's Questions about Death and Funerals*. Council Bluffs, IA: Centering Corp., 1980. An explanation of death, funerals, and saying good-bye.

Katherine S. Newman, *Hospice Coloring Book*. Hospice of Central FL, 1988. Just what the title says.

6) A teacher's son; and oriental children:

Pearl Buck, *The Big Wave*. NY: Scholastic, 1948. Two Chinese boys are friends, Jiya the son of fishing people and Kino the offspring of poor farmers. After a tidal wave kills all the fishing people on the shore, Jiya mourns, chooses to live with Kino's family (vs. adoption by a rich man), and eventually returns to the seaside with his bride, Kino's sister.

Eve Bunting, *The Happy Funeral*. NY: Harper & Row, 1982. A young Chinese-American girl prepares for her grandfather's funeral. A small candy after the ceremony to sweeten your sorrow?

Eleanor Coerr, *Sadako and the Thousand Paper Cranes*. NY: Putnam's, 1977. Based on a true story of a Japanese girl who died of leukemia in 1955 as one of the long-term outcomes of atomic bombing. A friend reminds her of the old legend that good health will be granted to a person who folds 1000 paper cranes. They begin the task and her classmates help, but she dies before the goal is reached.

Norma Simon, *We Remember Philip*. Chicago: Whitman, 1979. When the adult son of a male elementary school teacher dies in a mountain climbing accident, Sam and other members of his class inquire about what happened, observe how Mr. Hall is affected by his grief, share scrapbook and other memories, and plant a tree as a class memorial. An Afterword addresses the need of children to deal with and find reassurance for feelings that are personally threatening.

7) For middle and high school readers:

Fran Arrick, *Tunnel Vision.* Scarsdale, NY: Bradbury, 1980. When Anthony Hamil hangs himself at 15, his family (Mom, Dad, Denise), friends (Carl, Ditto, and Jane), and teacher cope with feelings of guilt and bewilderment. There is no easy resolution.

Judy Blume, *Tiger Eyes.* Scarsdale, NY: Bradbury, 1981. Davey's father is killed in the holdup of his 7-11 store in Atlantic City. Struggling with grief and out of synch with each other, Davey (15), her mother, and her younger brother move to Los Alamos, the "bomb city," to visit her father's sister. They stay almost a year before they find ways to move forward in mourning and decide to move back to New Jersey to pick up their lives once again.

John Coburn, *Annie and the Sand Dobbies: A Story about Death for Children and their Parents.* NY: Seabury, 1964. Danny's toddler sister dies in her sleep of a 'respiratory infection and his dog runs away to be found frozen to death. A neighbor uses imaginary characters to suggest that the deceased are safe with God.

Elfie Donnelly, *So Long, Grandpa.* NY: Crown, 1981. Michael at 10 witnesses the deterioration and eventual death from cancer of his grandfather. Portrays Michael's reactions and those of others, including the grandfather who prepares the boy by taking him to the funeral of an elderly friend.

Carol Farley, *The Garden Is Doing Fine.* NY: Atheneum, 1975. Why is 14-year-old Corrie's father dying of cancer? His interest in his garden leads to the realization that life goes on in his children.

Anne Frank, *The Diary of a Young Girl.* Celebrated story of the Dutch girl and her family who hide from the Nazi occupation of Holland in World War II.

C. Graeber, *Mustard.* NY: Macmillan, 1982. Mustard is a cat who belongs to 8-year-old Alex and his family. At 14, Mustard wants to be left alone some times; he does not like to be teased by Alex's sister, Annie, or upset by the paperboy's dog, Barney. In fact, Mustard is getting old, even though Alex refuses to admit that fact. The veterinarian confirms that Mustard's heart is not as strong as it used to be and recommends avoiding stress or excitement. One day, Mustard has a heart attack brought on by a confrontation with Barney. That night, he is unable to see or walk correctly; soon he cannot not eat, drink, or take his medicine. Finally, in order to relieve Mustard's pain the veterinarian helps him die in peace. The family buries Mustard in the back yard, keeps his collar and catnip mouse as mementos, and gives the rest of his things to the animal shelter. All of this is hard for Alex, but when he is offered a new cat he decides that he just isn't ready for that right now. A simple, clear, and unromanticized story of love, loss, and grief.

Jan Greenberg, *A Season In-Between.* NY: Farrar, 1979. Carrie Singer, a seventh grader, copes with the diagnosis of her father's cancer in spring and his death that summer. Rabbinical moral: turn scratches on a jewel into a beautiful design.

Constance C. Greene, *Beat the Turtle Drum.* NY: Viking, 1976. Most of this story describes a loving, warm family which includes 13-year-old Kate and 11-year-old Joss. When Joss is abruptly and unexpectedly killed in a fall from a tree, the family is flooded with grief. Conveying this sense of bereavement is the book's strong point.

Sharon Grollman, *Shira: A Legacy of Courage.* NY: Doubleday, 1988. Based on Shira's diary and letters.

Monica Hughes, *Hunter in the Dark.* NY: ATHENEUM, 1984. Mike Rankin is going hunting in the Canadian woods for the first time. He has leukemia (and overprotective parents) and needs to face life and death on his own.

Virginia Lee, *The Magic Moth.* NY: Seabury, 1972. Following an incurable heart disease, 5-year-old Mark-O's 10-year-old sister, Maryanne, dies. Mark-O is helped by the metaphor of the moth's transition from one mode of life to another. AV

Peggy Mann, *There Are Two Kinds of Terrible.* NY: Doubleday/Avon, 1977. Robbie breaks his arm and is hospitalized, but it ends. His mother develops cancer and dies. Robbie and his "cold fish" father grieve alone until they begin to find ways to come together in their suffering. Good vignettes, e.g., a substitute teacher threatens to call Robbie's mother when he misbehaves.

Katherine Paterson, *Bridge to Terabithia.* NY: Crowell, 1977. 11-year-old Jess and Leslie have their own special, secret meeting place in the woods, which they call "Terabithia". The magic of their play is disrupted when the girl is killed in an accident on the way to visit Terabithia alone. Sharing this special relationship leads to grief and to efforts to initiate new relationships of a similar sort with others.

Mary Francis Shura, *The Sunday Doll.* NY: Dodd, Mead, 1988. At the time of her 13th birthday, Emily is shut out from something terrible involving her older sister, Jayne (18). Her parents send Emily off to visit Aunt Harriet in Missouri, who had previously sent Emily an Amish doll without a face. Eventually, Emily learns that Jayne's boyfriend is missing; later he is found to have taken his life. Aunt Harriet suffers one of her "spells" (transient ischemia attacks) and comes close to death, but she also shows Emily her own strengths and that (like the Sunday doll) one can choose which face to present to the world. A richly textured story.

Doris Buchanan Smith, *A Taste of Blackberries.* NY: Scholastic, 1973. Tells the story of the death of Jamie, the narrator's best friend, as a result of an allergic reaction to a bee sting and the narrator's reflections on this unexpected event. "'Some questions do not have answers." AV

E. B. White, *Charlotte's Webb.* NY: Harper, 1952. Charlotte, the spider, spins fabulous webs to save Wilbur, Fern's pet pig, from the butcher's knife. In the end, Charlotte dies, but her babies live on. AV

Ruth Whitehead, *The Mother Tree.* NY: Seabury, 1971. Where do 11-year-old Tempe and her 4-year-old sister, Laura, turn to for comfort in the early 1900s when their mother dies and Tempe is promoted into the parental role? To a spiritual refuge in a large, old, backyard tree and eventually to memories.

8) Some classics:

James Agee, *A Death in the Family.* NY: Bantam, 1969.

Margaret Craven, *I Heard the Owl Call My Name.* NY: Dell, 1973. Novel about a young Episcopal priest who is sent to live with and learn from Indians in British Columbia who recognize that death will come when the owl calls.

John Gunther, *Death Be Not Proud.* NY: Harper, 1949. A moving account of a 15-month struggle with a brain tumor by the author's 15-year-old son. AV

C. S. Lewis, *A Grief Observed.* NY: Bantam, 1976. A famous author and lay theologian writes out his own grief at the death of his wife on notebooks around the house in such a direct and honest way that his experience has helped many thousands of readers. AV

Leo Tolstoy, *The Death of Ivan Ilych.* NY: New American Library, 1960.

9) Younger voices speak for themselves about dying and grief:

Jill Krementz, *How It Feels When a Parent Dies.* NY: Knopf, 1981. In short essays, 18 children and adolescents (7-16 years old) describe their reactions to a parent's death. Each essay is accompanied by a photograph of its author.

Edith Pendleton, *Too Old to Cry, Too Young to Die.* Nashville: Thomas Nelson, 1980. 35 teenagers describe their experiences in living with cancer: treatments, side effects, hospitals, parents, siblings, friends, etc.

Elizabeth Richter, *Losing Someone You Love: When a Brother or Sister Dies.* NY: Putnam, 1986. Fifteen adolescents describe in their own words how they are feeling in response to a wide variety of bereavement experiences. Many young people will find it important to know that they are not alone in these feelings of grief.

10) Books designed to teach:

Joanne E. Bernstein, *Loss: And How to Cope with It.* NY: Clarion, 1977. A warm, helpful book for young readers on how to cope with loss through death.

Margaret Coffin, *Death in Early America.* Nashville: Thomas Nelson, 1976. Cross-generational continuity in customs.

James Hamilton-Paterson & Carol Andrews, *Mummies: Death and Life in Ancient Egypt.* NY: Penguin, 1979. A specialized topic of widespread interest.

Elaine Landau, *Death: Everyone's Heritage.* NY: Messner, 1976. Information and viewpoints about medical death, euthanasia, care for the dying, suicide, cryonics, funerals, cemeteries, and survivors.

John Langone, *Death is a Noun & Vital Signs.* Boston: Little, Brown, 1972 & 1974. A medical reporter provides information and commentary for mature young readers about death in our society.

Robert Jay Lifton & Eric Olson, *Living and Dying.* NY: Bantam, 1974. An effective, popular presentation of complex concepts: connection/separation, movement/stasis, and integrity/disintegration. This leads to discussion of the nuclear age, holocausts, Vietnam, technology, and disintegrating values. The message: confront death, risk loss, and live well.

Sara Bonnett Stein, *About Dying: An Open Family Book for Parents and Children Together.* NY: Walker & Co., 1974. Photographs.

Richard Watts, *Straight Talk about Death with Young People.* Philadelphia: Westminster, 1975.

Herbert Zim & Sonia Bleeker, *Life and Death.* NY: Morrow, 1970. The first nonfiction book providing candid information for young readers about technical matters related to death, e.g., longevity, aging, determination of death, funeral customs around the world, etc.

11) Bibliographical and other resource books:

Hannelore Wass, et al., *Death Education: An Annotated Resource Guide,* vols. I & II. Washington, DC: Hemisphere, 1980 & 1985. Annotated bibliographies of various sorts of resources, including children's literature in Vol. II.

Hannelore Wass & Charles A. Corr, *Helping Children Cope with Death: Guidelines and Resources.* Washington, DC: Hemisphere, 2nd ed. 1984.

Hannelore Wass & Charles A. Corr, *Childhood and Death.* Washington, DC: Hemisphere, 1984.

Charles A. Corr & Joan N. McNeil, *Adolescence and Death.* NY: Springer, 1986. All three are useful guides for students and helpers in their respective fields, and all contain annotated guides to literature for young people and for adults.

Joanne Bernstein, *Books to Help Children Cope with Separation and Loss.* NY: Bowker, 1978; 2nd ed. 1984; vol. 3 = 1989. Wide topical range; very helpful descriptions, evaluations, and ratings. Bibliotherapy.

The Rainbow Connection/Compassionate Book Service, 477 Hannah Branch Road, Burnsville, NC 28714. (704) 675-5909. Maintains a current collection of resources for children and caregivers on illness, loss and grief.

Selected and Annotated Bibliographies

Charles A. Corr

Children and Death

Two basic resources are: *Childhood & Death* (1984) & *Helping Children Cope with Death: Guidelines and Resources* (2nd ed., 1984), ed. H. Wass & C.A. Corr (Washington, DC: Hemisphere). For adolescents, see C.A. Corr & J.N. McNeil (eds.), *Adolescence & Death* (NY: Springer, 1986).

A fine early book for parents and educators is *They Need to Know: How to Teach Children About Death* by A.K. Gordon & D. Klass (Englewood Cliffs, NJ: Prentice-Hall, 1979). Other efforts to assist parents are: C.L. Jewett, *Helping Children Cope with Separation and Loss* (Harvard, MA: Harvard Common Press, 1982); E.N. Jackson, *Telling a Child About Death* (NY: Hawthorn, 1965), & D. Schaefer & C. Lyons, *How Do We Tell the Children* (NY: Newmarket, 1986). See also J.E. Bernstein and M.K. Rudman, *Books to Help Children Cope with Separation and Loss* (Vol. 3; NY: Bowker, 1989). Resources for teachers are described in H.Wass, et al., *Death Education: An Annotated Resource Guide* (Washington, DC: Hemisphere, Vol. I, 1980, & Vol. II, 1985).

R. Lonetto looks at *Children's Conceptions of Death* (NY: Springer, 1980) developmentally, while M. Bluebond-Langner explores life experiences in *The Private Worlds of Dying Children* (Princeton, NJ: Princeton U. Press, 1978).

Four good books address care of children & families coping with cancer: D.W. Adams, *Childhood Malignancy: The Psychsocial Care of the Child and His Family* (Springfield, IL: Charles C Thomas, 1979); G.P. Koocher & J.E. O'Malley, *The Damocles Syndrome* (NY: McGraw-Hill, 1981); J.J. Spinetta & P. Deasy-Spinetta, *Living with Childhood* Cancer (St. Louis: Mosby, 1981): & D.W. Adams & E.J. Deveau, *Coping with Childhood Cancer: Where Do We Go From Here?* (rev. ed.; Hamilton, Ontario: Kinbridge, 1987).

Hospice Approaches to Pediatric Care, ed. C.A. Corr & D.M. Corr (NY: Springer, 1985), *Pediatric Hospice Care: What Helps*, ed. B. Martin (Los Angeles: Childrens Hospital, 1989), & *Hospice Care for Children*, ed. A. Armstrong-Dailey & S.Z. Goltzer (NY: Oxford U. Press, 1993) offer hospice perspectives on caring for dying or bereaved children & their families. See also R.W. Buckingham, *A Special Kind of Love: Care of the Dying Child* (NY: Continuum, 1983).

I. Martinson's *Home Care for the Dying Child: Professional & Family Perspectives* (NY:

Appleton-Century-Crofts, 1976) is a pioneer in its field. Martinson's Home Care Project also produced *Home Care: A Manual for the Implementation of Home Care for Children Dying of Cancer* & *Home Care: A Manual for Parents* (Minneapolis: U. of Minnesota, School of Nursing, 1978 & 1979).

Ill & bereaved children speak for themselves in: E. Pendleton (comp.), *Too Old to Cry, Too Young to Die* (Nashville, TN: Thomas Nelson, 1980), & J. Krementz, *How It Feels When a Parent Dies* (NY: Knopf, 1981). For advice to such children: E. LeShan, *Learning to Say Good-by: When a Parent Dies* (NY: Macmillan, 1976), & J.E. Bernstein, *Loss & How to Cope with It* (NY: Seabury, 1977). *A Child's Parent Dies* by E. Furman (New Haven: Yale U. Press, 1974) is a classic. See also: H. Rosen, *Unspoken Grief: Coping with Childhood Sibling Loss* (Lexington, MA: Heath, 1986), K.F. Donnelly, *Recovering From the Loss of a Parent* (NY: Dodd, Mead, 1987), & N.B. Webb, *Helping Bereaved Children: A Handbook for Practitioners* (NY: Guilford, 1993).

See also: two anthologies entitled, *The Child & Death*—one edited by O.J. Sahler (St. Louis: Mosby, 1978), the other by J.E. Schowalter, et al. (NY: Columbia U. Press, 1983); J.E. Gyulay, *The Dying Child* (NY: McGraw-Hill, 1978); & three volumes from conferences: *Children & Death,* ed. G.H. Patterson (London, Ont.: King's College, 1986), *The Dying & Bereaved Teenager,* ed. J.D. Morgan (Phil.: The Charles Press, 1990), & *Young People and Death,* ed. J.D. Morgan (Phil.: The Charles Press, 1991). Finally, E. Kübler-Ross, *On Children & Death* & *AIDS: The Ultimate Challenge* (NY: Macmillan, 1983 & 1987).

Parents writing in bereavement include: J. Claypool, *Tracks of a Fellow Struggler: How to Handle Grief* (Waco, TX: Word Books, 1974); N. Roach, *The Last Days of April* (Washington, DC: American Cancer Society, 1974); A.A. Smith, *Rachel* (Wilton, CT: Morehouse-Barlow, 1974); & R. Stinson & P. Stinson, *The Long Dying of Baby Andrew* (Boston: Little, Brown, 1983).

M.S. Miles, *The Grief of Parents When a Child Dies,* is a helpful booklet (The Compassionate Friends, P.O. Box 1347, Oak Brook, IL 60521). See also: S. Stephens, *Death Comes Home* (Wilton, CT: Morehouse-Barlow, 1973); H.S. Schiff, *The Bereaved Parent* (NY: Crown, 1977); K.F. Donnelly in *Recovering From the Loss of a Child* (NY: Macmillan, 1982); J.H. Arnold & P.B. Gemma, *A Child Dies: A Portrait of Family Grief* (Rockville, MD: Aspen, 1983); T.A. Rando (ed.), *Parental Loss of a Child* (Champaign, IL: Research Press, 1986); R.J. Knapp, *Beyond Endurance: When a Child Dies* (NY: Schocken, 1986); S. Johnson, *After a Child Dies: Counseling Bereaved Families* (NY: Springer, 1987); & D. Klass, *Parental Grief: Solace and Resolution* (NY: Springer, 1989).

Eight books on early childhood death are: C.A. Corr, et al. (eds.), *Sudden Infant Death Syndrome: Who Can Help and How,* (NY: Springer, 1991); J. DeFrain, et al., *Sudden Infant Death: Enduring the Loss* (Lexington, MA: Heath, 1991); S. Borg, & J. Lasker, *When Pregnancy Fails: Families Coping with Miscarriage, Still birth, & Infant Death* (Boston: Beacon, 1981); J. DeFrain, J. Taylor, & L. Ernst, *Coping with Sudden Infant Death* (Boston: Beacon, 1982); J. DeFrain, et al., *Stillborn: The Invisible Death* (Heath, 1986); S.L.M. Jimenez, *The Other Side of Pregnancy: Coping with Miscarriage*

& *Stillbirth* (Englewood Cliffs, NJ: Prentice-Hall, 1982); B. Knight, *Sudden Death in Infancy: The 'Cot Death' Syndrome* (London: Faber & Faber, 1983); & L.G. Peppers, & R.J. Knapp, *Motherhood and Mourning: Perinatal Death* (NY: Praeger, 1980).

For suicide, see: F. Klagsbrun, *Too Young to Die, Youth & Suicide* (Boston: Houghton, Mifflin, 1976; NY: Pocket Books, 1977); P. Giovacchini, *The Urge to Die: Why Young People Commit Suicide* (NY: Macmillan, 1981); & *Youth Suicide* (NY: Springer, 1985), edited by M.L. Peck, N.L. Farberow, & R.E. Litman. Note also J.H. Hewett, *After Suicide* (Phil.: Westminster Press, 1980).

General accounts of grief & bereavement include: J.W. Worden, *Grief Counseling & Grief Therapy: A Handbook for the Mental Health Practitioner* (2nd ed., NY: Springer, 1991); B. Raphael, *The Anatomy of Bereavement* (NY: Basic Books, 1983); T.A. Rando, *Grief, Dying, & Death: Clinical Interventions for Caregivers* (Champaign, IL: Research Press, 1984); T.A. Rando, *Grieving* (Lexington, MA: Heath, 1988); & C.A. Sanders, *Grief: The Mourning After* (NY: John Wiley, 1989).

Two new resources for counseling children include Nancy Boyd Well's *Helping Bereaved Children* (NY: Guilford, 1993) and W. Warden's *When a Parent Dies: Counseling Bereaved Children* (NY: Guilford, 1995).

Adolescence and Death

The literature on adolescent development & issues faced by adolescents is quite extensive. Two examples are *Adolescent development: Early through Late adolescence* (Pacific Grove, CA: Brooks/Cole, 1995), by D.E. Balk, & *The adolescent: A psychological self-portrait* (NY: Basic Books, 1981), by D. Offer, E. Ostrov, & K.I. Howard.

For issues related to death, see *Adolescence and death* (NY: Springer, 1986), ed. C.A. Corr & J.N. McNeil. And look for *Helping adolescents cope with death and bereavement* ed. C.A. Corr & D.E. Balk (NY: Springer, 1995?).

Adolescents (& children) write about life-threatening illness in E. Pendleton (Comp.), *Too old to cry, too young to die* (Nashville, TN: Thomas Nelson, 1980), & J. Krementz, *How it feels to fight for your life* (Boston: Little, Brown, 1989).

Adolescents (& children) discuss bereavement in J. Krementz, *How it feels when a parent dies* (NY: Knopf, 1981), & E. Richter, *Losing someone you love: When a brother or sister dies* (NY: Putnam, 1986). See also: H. Rosen, *Unspoken Grief: Coping with Childhood Sibling Loss* (Lexington, MA: Heath, 1986). K.F. Donnelly, *Recovering From the Loss of a Parent* (NY: Dodd, Mead, 1987), L. La Grand, *Coping with separation and loss as a young adult: Theoretical and practical realities* (Springfield, IL: Charles C Thomas, 1986); & a special issue of the *Journal of Adolescent Research* Vol. 6, No. 1; 1991) on "death and adolescent bereavement," ed. D.E. Balk.

There is a large body of literature on suicide and life-threatening behavior among adolescents. For example: Alcohol, Drug Abuse, and Mental Health Administration, *Report of the secretary's task force on youth suicide* (4 vols.; Washington, DC: U.S. Government Printing Office, 1989); L. Coleman, *Suicide clusters* (Boston: Faber & Faber, 1987); P. Giovacchini, *The urge to die: Why young people commit suicide* (NY: Macmillan, 1981); F. Klagsbrun, *Too young to die: Youth and suicide* (NY: Houghton Mifflin, 1976; Pocket Books, 1977); D. Lester, *The cruelest death: The enigma of adolescent suicide* (Philadelphia: The Charles Press, 1993); & M.L. Peck, N.L. Farberow, & R.E. Litman (Eds.), *Youth suicide* (NY: Springer, 1985). See also J.E. Mack & H. Hickler, *Vivienne: The life and suicide of an adolescent girl* (Boston: Little, Brown, 1981).

Advice is offered to bereaved adolescents in: R. Watts, *Straight talk about death with young people* (Philadelphia: Westminster, 1975); E. LeShan, *Learning to Say Good-by: When a Parent Dies* (NY: Macmillan, 1976; Avon, 1978); J.E. Bernstein, *Loss & How To Cope with It* (NY: Seabury, 1977); K. Gravelle & C. Haskins, *Teenagers face to face with bereavement* (NY: Julian Messner, 1989); J. Bode, *Death is hard to live with: Teenagers and how they cope with death* (NY: Delacorte, 1993); & E.A. Grollman, *Straight talk about death for teenagers: How to cope with losing someone you love* (Boston: Beacon Press, 1993). See also, G. Baxter, L. Bennett, & W. Stuart, *Adolescents and death: Bereavement support groups for secondary school students* (2nd ed., Etobicoke, Ontario: Canadian Centre for Death Education and Bereavement at Humber College, 1989).

Teaching adolescents about death is discussed by F. Sternberg & B. Sterberg, *If I die and when I do: Exploring death with young people* (Englewood Cliffs, NJ: Prentice-Hall, 1980), & by A.K. Gordon & D. Klass, *They need to know: How to teach children about death* (Englewood Cliffs, NJ: Prentice-Hall, 1979). See also J.E. Bernstein & M.K. Rudman, *Books to help children cope with separation and loss* (Vol. 3; NY: Bowker, 1989).

For crisis intervention, see: T.N. Fairchild (Ed.), *Crisis intervention strategies for school-based helpers.* (Springfield, IL: Charles C Thomas, 1986), & A.A. Leenaars & S. Wenckstern (Eds.), *Suicide prevention in the schools* (Washington, DC: Hemisphere, 1991).

J.D. Morgan has edited two collections of articles on children and adolescents: *The dying & bereaved teenager & Young people & death* (both = Philadelphia: The Charles Press, 1990 & 1991).

The bibliography is restricted to book-length publications since the journal literature is too vast to survey briefly. Readers should also consult reviews & articles in the pediatric, thanatological, & hospice journals. Even with many limitations, there clearly are a large number of relevant books. But no book is right for all readers & purposes. Individuals must keep up to date & assess for themselves which are the most valuable titles.

Some Books to Guide Adults in Talking about Death with Children

Bernstein, J.E., & Rudman, M.K. (1989). *Books to Help Children Cope with Separation and Loss,* Vol. 3. New York: Bowker. (Vol. 1 = 1978; Vol. 2 = 1984). These three volumes contain informed and sensitive descriptions of a very large number of books for children. They cover a broad range of topics and offer keen evaluations of each title listed. They also advocate and explain at length ways in which to use books to help children cope with loss and grief. An excellent reference source.

Gordon, A.K., & Klass, D. (1979). *They Need to Know: How to Teach Children About Death.* Englewood Cliffs, NJ: Prentice-Hall. Goals, strategies, and materials for teaching children about death at each grade level from pre-school through high school. A fine guide for teachers and parents.

Grollman, E.A. (1990). *Talking About Death: A Dialogue Between Parent and Child* (3rd ed.). Boston: Beacon Press. There are four major sections in this book: a set of principles for helping children to cope with death; a passage which an adult should read along with a child; a lengthy guide to responding to questions that may naturally arise in the read-along section; and a guide to helpful resources. A classic in this field.

Heegard, M. (1988). *When Someone Very Special Dies.* Minneapolis: Woodland. A story line for children to illustrate or color. Open-ended and practical.

Jackson, E.N. (1965). *Telling a Child About Death.* New York: Hawthorn. An older, but still useful, guide for adults. Slim, but helpful.

Jewett, C.L. (1982). *Helping Children Cope with Separation and Loss.* Harvard, MA: Harvard Common Press. Useful advice for adults from a child and family therapist.

Johnson, J., & Johnson, M. (1980). *Tell Me, Papa: A Family Book for Children's Questions About Death and Funerals.* Council Bluffs, IA: Centering Corporation. One of many, little pocketbooks from this Iowa resource center. Explains death, funerals, and saying good-bye.

Schaefer, D., & Lyons, C. (1986). *How Do We Tell the Children: A Parent's Guide to Helping Children Understand and Cope When Someone Dies.* New York: Newmarket. A New York funeral director and his co-author offer practical advice for parents. (There is a revised edition of this book.)

Wolfelt, A. (1983). *Helping Children Cope with Grief.* Muncie, IN: Accelerated Development. A well-known educator and clinical psychologist writes about advice, suggested activities, and resources for helping grieving children.

Audrey Harris, *Why Did He Die?* Minneapolis: Lerner, 1965. A mother explains death to her young son whose friend's grandfather has died. Question and answer format; aging, the life cycle, memories, quality of life.

Barbara S. Hazen, *Why Did Grandpa Die? A Book about Death.* NY: Golden, 1985. Young Molly and her grandfather have much in common. When Grandpa dies suddenly, Molly cannot accept this harsh fact and does not feel like crying. Her father reminds her that Grandpa was also his father whom he loved very much. Many things remind Molly of how much she misses Grandpa. It takes a long time to acknowledge that he will not come back.

Linda Peavy, *Allison's Grandfather.* NY: Chas. Scribner's Sons, 1981. Erica thinks about his friend's grandfather (on his ranch) while he is dying. Momma holds his hand as he dies.

Jennifer Bartoli, *Nonna.* NY: Harvey House, 1975. A boy and his younger sister have good memories of being with Grandma on her swing and of her cookies. They are involved in her funeral, burial, and settling her affairs.

Charlotte Zolotow, *My Grandson Lew.* NY: Harper, 1974. Lewis awakens in the night and wonders why his grandfather has not visited recently. The mother had not told her son that the grandfather is dead because he hadn't asked. The boy says that he hadn't needed to ask; his grandfather just came. They share warm memories of someone they both miss, e.g., "he gave me eye hugs." "Now we will remember him together and neither of us will be so lonely as we would be if we had to remember him alone." (Loss shared is eased.) AV

Andrea F. Clardy, *Dusty Was My Friend: Coming to Terms with Loss.* Human Sciences, 1984. Benjamin (8) remembers his friend Dusty (10), who was killed in a car accident, and tries to understand his feelings about losing a friend in this way.

Janice Cohn, *I Had a Friend Named Peter.* NY: Wm. Morrow, 1987. Beth's friend, Peter, is killed by a car; her parents & teacher answer questions.

Jean Little, *Mama's Going to Buy You a Mockingbird.* NY: Viking Kestrel, 1984. Jeremy and his younger sister, Sarah, only learn that their father is dying from cancer by overhearing someone talking about it. Lack of information and limited contacts when he is in the hospital leave the children confused and angry. Two central themes in this story are: the many losses, large and small, that accompany dying and death; and the need for support from others.

E. Sandy Powell, *Geranium Morning.* Minneapolis: CarolRhoda Books, 1990. This is the story of two young children: Timothy, whcse father died suddenly in an accident, and Frannie, whose mother is dying. The children struggle with strong feelings, memories, guilt ("if onlys"), and some unhelpful adult actions. But they also are helped by Frannie's father and by her mother before she dies. Above all, in sharing their losses, the two children help each other.

Joan S. Prestine, *Someone Special Died.* LA: Price/Stern/Sloan, 1987. Attitudes in grief; memories.

Doris Sanford, *It Must Hurt a Lot.* Portland, OR: Multnomah Press, 1986. Anya's reactions to a death and realizations (secrets) about what such reactions teach.

Contributors

Paul Alexander is a social worker at St. Mary's Hospice for Children in New York and is a composer, performer, and recording artist of songs about children's grief. His music is widely used in training and therapy sessions for caregivers, as well as with children.

Gary R. Anderson is an Associate Professor at Hunter College School of Social Work at the City University of New York. He was a pioneer on matters relating to children and HIV and has written frequently about the needs of children with HIV and their families.

Ronald K. Barrett is Associate Professor of Psychology at Loyola Marymount University and is a bereavement consultant to education and government agencies in California. His research has focused on the effects of violence on children.

Charles A. Corr, one of America's leading educators on death education, is Professor of Philosophy at Southern Illinois University and the author of many books on children and death, adolescents and death, hospice, and Sudden Infant Death Syndrome (SIDS).

Kenneth J. Doka is Professor of Gerontology at the College of New Rochelle, past president of the Association for Death Education and Counseling, a sociologist, and a Lutheran pastor. He is editor of *Journeys*, a newsletter to help in bereavement, published by the Hospice Foundation of America.

Earl A. Grollman, a rabbi, is a noted lecturer on bereavement topics, a frequent guest on TV and radio shows to discuss questions of death and dying education, and is the author of many books, including *Explaining Death to Children* and *Straight Talk About Death for Teenagers*.

Stephen P. Hersh is founder and director of the Medical Illness Counseling Center, a non-profit institution working with the chronically and terminally ill. He is clinical professor of psychiatry, behavioral sciences, and pediatrics at George Washington University Medical School and contributing editor of *Journeys*.

Catherine M. Sanders is a psychologist in general practice and director of The Center for the Study of Separation and Loss. She is a prominent researcher in grief matters and among her writings are *Grief: The Mourning After* and *Surviving Grief and Learning to Live Again*.

Robert G. Stevenson, a death educator and grief counselor, has taught a death education course for over 20 years at the high school level. He is co-chairman of the Seminar on Death at Columbia University and has written widely on topics related to loss and grief.

ORDER FORM

Children Mourning, Mourning Children

Edited by Kenneth J. Doka, Ph.D. $14.95

ISBN: 1-56032-447-3

For bulk quantity orders, call Hospice Foundation of America
1-800-854-3402
or write Hospice Foundation of America
    Suite 300, 2001 S Street, NW
    Washington, DC 20009

For single copies, write Taylor & Francis

Payment Options

_____ Enclosed is my check or money order, payable to Taylor & Francis, in U.S. funds only.

Please charge my ____ Visa ____ MC ____ Amex

Card #_____Exp. _____

Signature _____

Telephone *(required for credit card purchase)* _____

P.O.#_____ Date _____

Bill/Ship to

Name _____

Institution _____

Address _____

_____

City_____State_____Zip _____

_____ Subtotal   _____ Shipping & Handling**

_____ Sales Tax (PA only)   _____ Total

**Add $2.50 for book orders $50 and under.

Send Order Form To:
    Taylor & Francis
    1900 Frost Road, Suite 101
    Bristol, PA 19007-1598

TO ORDER BY PHONE, CALL TOLL FREE 1-800-821-8312
Or send orders on our 24-hour telefax, 215-785-5515

Orders can also be placed via the Internet at bkorders@tandfpa.com